# Normality is Hard W[...]

## Trade Unions
## Politics of Con[...]

**Mick Carpenter**

*Lawrence & Wishart*
London

Lawrence & Wishart
144a Old South Lambeth Road
London SW8 1XX

First published 1994 by Lawrence & Wishart
© Mick Carpenter 1994

Text and cover design by Jan Brown Designs
Illustrations by Angela Martin
Printed and bound in Great Britain by Redwood Books, Trowbridge

*Maintaining normality is hard work: a body must be rested, cleaned, groomed, and clothed every day; it must be fed properly and decorously at the correct time and it must be made to walk the right tracks and talk the right things... Whatever becomes a possibility for many turns into a necessity for everyone. If some physical defect or affliction can be cured, it must be. If a majority can read, the others thereby become illiterates who must also be taught to read and write. If running water becomes generally available, it puts everybody under constant pressure to wash.*
(Abram de Swaan, 1990, p1)

## Acknowledgments

I am grateful to COHSE, which is now part of UNISON, who initially encouraged me to undertake the research which has led to this book. On the way I have received help and support from many people, including Bob Aberley, Sarah Copsey, Sally Davison, Cristine Durrance, Helen Findlay, Jenny Frieze, Scott Goodfellow, John Goodman, John Harris, Karen Jennings, Richard Parker, Robert Quick, Jayne Simpson, Vyomesh Thanki, Pam Wood, and Ali Worthy. Responsibility for accuracy and for the views expressed is of course mine, and they are not a statement of UNISON policy.

# Contents

# Foreword

UNISON is publishing this book to draw attention to the importance of community care as an issue, both to our own members and to the public at large. We do not seek to endorse every point it argues, some of which are bound to be controversial. In commissioning this exploration of the politics of trade unionism and community care set in its historical context, we gave its author complete freedom and independence to develop and present his views. Its publication is therefore consistent with the spirit of openness which characterises UNISON as a self-aware and innovative organisation, seeking to stimulate internal debate and reach out to the wider community.

The 1990 Community Care Act established the right of infirm and disabled people to live as independently as possible in their own homes. It laid down procedures for assessing people's individual needs for home or residential care, with the involvement of users and carers, to enable them to receive the means of support they required to participate in the life of the community. It was the first time since the welfare state was created after World War 2, that such rights had been enshrined in a major piece of legislation.

Sadly, as Mick Carpenter shows in this book commissioned by UNISON, there is a considerable gap between the rhetoric of these reforms and how they are likely to operate in practice. While purporting to uplift the status and dignity of users and carers, and establishing rights to services, they are in reality intended to be an effective 'cap' on community care expenditure which will inevitably lead to rationing. At the same time this will enforce the privatisation of services so creating a replica of the 'internal market' within local authority community care which has proved so disastrous in the NHS. The book shows that the 1990 NHS and community care reforms are part of a grand design to streamline acute care in the NHS, and to offload and cheapen care altogether. In this context the community care reforms can be seen as a poison chalice which has been passed to local authorities to implement. Insufficient and cash limited resources have been made available to implement the measures in full. The managerialist and marketised model advocated is inappropriate to the caring sector, and the wider supportive social policies and anti-discriminatory measures which are also needed are nowhere in sight. When the reforms fail there is no doubt that the government will seek to blame local authorities – especially one so reluctant to take any responsibility for its own mistakes.

Does this mean that the reforms are simply another Tory con-trick, which should therefore be opposed by all right minded people? Mick Carpenter is emphatic that this is not the case, and that there is a progressive core to the reforms, which must be both defended and transformed. If this is so, it is only there because it was campaigned for from below by user groups, trades unionists – not least in UNISON and its predecessors – and others. Since the early 1980s we have protested vigorously against the dogmatic Thatcherite determination to simply pitch people out of public institutions in the expectation that hard-pressed families would take the strain, while at the same time unashamedly fuelling the massive and unregulated growth of private institutional care.

The general arguments in favour of what Mick Carpenter calls 'user centred and worker friendly' community care are ones which many members of UNISON and, hopefully, other people in the world beyond would support; also his insistence that services organised upon these lines need to be developed within a supportive framework of egalitarian social and economic policies. The pursuit of policies such as these is far from the mind of the present government. It is intent on driving down the pay and conditions of users, and putting people's rights to services in question, in order to deal with the massive budget deficit it has created. This time around we must ensure that the attempt to divide workers from users, which will no doubt be mounted in order to deflect attention from the disastrous mistakes of the last fourteen years, is not successful. To prevent this happening we must find ways of acknowledging and addressing genuine differences of interest, while at the same time forging effective alliances to defend and improve services for the benefit of service users and employees alike. Realising our future vision of responsive, high quality, well-managed, democratically run, and individually sensitive public services which also meet the aspirations of employed workers, is the central task to which UNISON has dedicated itself in the years leading up to the next century. Within this overall aim, giving high priority to the development of 'good' community care will be crucial, and UNISON hopes that the publication of this book will help to stimulate wide debate on how this might be best achieved.

**Alan Jinkinson**
UNISON General Secretary

# Introduction
# Towards user-centred and worker-friendly services

The aim of this book is to generate debate and discussion among the left, the labour movement and beyond, about future policies for community care. In all the furore generated by the shift to the internal market in health associated with the NHS reforms, the community care reforms which were an integral part of the 1990 NHS and Community Care Act have been largely overlooked, except by those directly affected by them. My concern below is how and in what ways community care can be made a central political issue, and services campaigned for that, unlike the 1990 Act, genuinely prioritise the needs and rights of users, both individually and collectively, while also respecting employed workers' legitimate interests.

The book insists that this can not be achieved by vague and rhetorical calls on workers and users to 'unite and fight'. There are many points of potential common interest between providers and users, and the community care reforms will be criticised for an approach to power which implies that it can only be enhanced by one party at the expense of another. However uniting users and providers can only occur if the latter accept the need for radical changes in existing services which have subordinated users in ways which at best have been paternalistic and at worse led to oppression and abuse. The tendency however until recently has been for producers' organisations to put any problems down to a shortfall in resources and to demand 'more of the same'. A different kind of unity to this must be constructed, based on recognition and respect for different needs and interests among the parties involved in care, while prioritising those of users – hence a 'user-centred and worker friendly' approach.

A simple producer-user divide, such as that which informs the 1990 community care reforms is unhelpful and misleading. First because services are hierarchically organised in ways that cause conflicts of interest among paid workers, between managers, professionals and front line workers and this is reinforced by the shift to contracting out. A precondition of a shift to user centred and worker friendly services is a fairer distribution of internal power which recognises the contribution, and provides opportunities for advancement, of all paid workers. Though this will help to make them worker friendly, it will not of itself however make them more user centred unless there is a corresponding shift in power to users. And when talking of users, we must not confuse them with unwaged carers. Improving the lot of carers is really a function of worker friendliness, while user centredness is about prioritising the needs of people who require care.

People can not be empowered within services if they are denied power in their wider lives. Nevertheless a hallmark of non oppressive services is that they do not make this an excuse for doing nothing, and seek to find ways of fulfiling the legitimate needs and rights of all parties through democratised public services. This gives rise to an alternative and more three dimensional concept of 'pluralistic' services to that embodied in the community care reforms, which simply suggests that competition between a 'plurality' of state, commercial and voluntary providers will lead to user sensitive care.

The fundamental principle underlying user centred and worker friendly care is that of a choice to care on both sides. If people feel themselves forced to care in circumstances that most of us would regard as unsatisfactory, either because they have no alternative employment opportunities or are pressured by imposed family obligations then this is not only an infringement of their rights but will set up conflicts that will lead to resentment and even abuse. This is not to argue against a general social obligation to care, but it must be fairly shared rather than imposed (particularly on women) and is a collective as well as individual obligation. Similarly those who need care have a right, provided they can exercise it, to choose who will care for them rather than to accept necessarily or ideally that this will be a family member, and society has a responsibility to make that choice available. In other words care must be 'disaggregated' and seen as a genuinely individual right, and to argue this is to take individualism much further than the current reforms. It is an optimistic approach. The new right fear that people will abandon caring responsibilities if they have such choices made available to them. In most instances they will not, and freely chosen care will be good for everyone, and help to remove some of the conflicts of interest caused on both sides by the relations of dependency associated with care.

This approach takes the guiding philosophy of the 'new' community care, as stated by the 1989 White Paper, *Caring for People*, which led to the 1990 reforms, to its logical conclusion:

Community care means providing the services and support which people who are affected by problems of ageing, mental illness, mental handicap or physical or sensory disability need to be able to live as independently as possible in their own homes, or in 'homely' settings in the community.

**4**

*Normality is hard work*

Within this ideal community care is not in itself a set of services or therapeutic practices but a means to an end, the social right to partici- pate in rather than be excluded from the life of the community.

If this ambitious goal is to be realised it will necessarily involve a radical approach to the empowerment of users, who in future must have the most significant say in deciding their own needs, through what it has become usual to call 'self advocacy'. Self-advocacy has been defined as 'a process in which an individual or a group of people, speak or act on their own be- half in pursuit of their needs and interests' (MIND, 1992a). Within this ap- proach the paid worker becomes an 'advocate', defined by Jim Read and Jan Wallcraft (1992) as one who seeks to support users in developing their own voice, only speaking on their behalf when they genuinely cannot do so. This new model will require concerted efforts to move beyond a 'part- nership' approach, which still tends to put employed workers and pro- fessionals in the driving seat. Following this road will inevitably be some- times fraught with difficulty, but it is the right and proper course.

This book seeks to put the current debates about strategy within their historical context. It argues that the 'managerial consumerist' or the 'new public management' (Hunter, 1993) approach was right to identify the fail- ure of the welfare state in the past to place users' needs and interests at the centre, but this was only partly the fault of a 'producer led' profession- alised and bureaucratic welfare state. Ironically for the new right, institu- tional bias and producer domination goes back to the period when 'Vic- torian values' reigned supreme, when large numbers of 'deviant' people, either with presumed or real disabilities, were incarcerated in institutions which were inherited by the welfare state. The failure of the welfare state has been its inability fully to replace this inheritance through a radical re- organisation of public services which prioritised users' rights and choices. The 1990 reforms promise therefore to address real deficiencies but will not deliver them because of the dominant managerialist-consumerist ap- proach, and its hidden agenda of privatisation. However the left and the labour movement need to do more than simply campaign for more re- sources to make the new form of community care work, and an end to pri- vatisation, it must face up to the failures of the past and seek to develop a more radical approach based on 'user centred and worker friendly' prin- ciples of empowerment.

I do not claim that this approach to trade unionism and the politics of community care will mean striking out in an entirely new direction. Each of the three unions which combined to form UNISON as the largest pub- lic services union in Europe in July 1993 – the Confederation of Health Ser- vice Employees (COHSE), the National and Local Government Officers' Association (NALGO) and the National Union of Public Employees (NUPE) – have in the 1980s increasingly shifted to a 'user-centred' approach to community care. However the aim is to make this approach more explicit, in ways that will facilitate the emergence of a progressive alliance for community care, as frustration mounts over the inability of the new system set up in 1990 to fulfil its promise.

## Bridging the Worker-User Divide

The political dangers of failing to go boldly down this road are only too apparent. Since the so-called Winter of Discontent of 1978-9 onwards, Conservative rule has in part been perpetuated by tapping user hostility to public sector workers. Like other divide-and-rule strategies it is not a complete political fabrication, but has some basis in people's material experience. The 1990 community care reforms are a continuing and significant example of this strategy. The 1988 Griffiths Report on which the 1990 reforms are based blamed the oppressive character and institutional bias of services on their being 'producer-led' within a system of state monopoly and professionally controlled provision. It was a simplistic analysis with simplistic solutions attached – that family care is best and that the commercial and voluntary sectors are inherently more user-sensitive alternatives. As we shall see, this ignores the historical evidence which shows that an oppressive institutional bias was imposed from outside by powerful social forces acting on the state. It also ignores the fact that smaller institutions run by commercial and even voluntary organisations are just as capable of a 'warehousing' or controlling approach and that care within the family – when it is available – is often associated with social isolation and sometimes oppression and abuse.

Nevertheless state workers have often acted in controlling and even abusive ways, and the underpinning of such services by professional power meant this oppression was often disguised as help, even when it was imposed against the will of those receiving it. If employed workers are to build new and effective alliances with users, they must acknowledge that in the past trade unions have been accomplices in such an indefensible system, and bear their share of responsibility for the slow progress towards community care before the 1980s.

The labour movement and the left have often been reluctant to admit to the existence of oppressive and abusive features of state services, or at best have blamed them on funding difficulties. They have often depicted state health and welfare services with a 'statist' ideology as a beneficial 'social wage' which must be defended at all costs. Even when left writers realise that many state services are a mixed blessing, they do so grudgingly. For example, Erik Wright and Donmoon Cho (1992) argue that there is a division in the state apparatus between 'the capitalist political superstructure' which through the courts, military, police and so on is primarily concerned with shoring up the system, and 'decommodified state services' which, though to some extent playing this role, 'should be regarded as also constituting elements of an *embryonic post-capitalist mode of production* located within the state' (original emphasis).

Expressed without use of Marxist jargon, this means that they should be regarded as addressing people's needs as users, less restrained by the requirements of the economic system. Unfortunately, that is often not how they have been perceived by those at the receiving end of those state services which are now targeted for community care reform. Such a statist bias on the left has often dovetailed with a 'workerism' by trade unions in the public services. At best this has led to a narrow focus on pay and conditions, and at worst campaigns to defend institutions and oppressive services. It is also to accept implicitly the artificial division and polarisation of people's needs as employed workers on the one hand, and as users and carers on the other. In fact union members are not solely 'workers' but also users of public services who would benefit from a shift in services in a user centred direction.

I argue below on the basis of historical evidence that we should acknowledge more explicitly that these were services which were much more concerned with controlling users than addressing their social and personal needs. If we identify such services as proto-socialist simply because they are 'decommodified', we encourage their negative features to be associated with socialism and trade unionism. This in turn makes them a ready target for 'recommodification' through consumerism and privatisation, as supposedly non-oppressive alternatives. Like it or not, the community care reforms in such a context represent a form of analysis and practical programme which, though misleading and ultimately wrong-headed, are more in tune with people's direct experiences than that often offered by the left and the labour movement.

## Why the 1990 Reforms Have Not Been More Controversial

This is one significant reason why the 1990 community care reforms have generated much less controversy and opposition than the NHS reforms, even though they will involve a much more extensive programme of privatisation. The ideological bracketing of socialism and professionalism with the oppressive institutional bias of services, contrasted by competition, choice and user empowerment has a greater legitimacy. By its past inaction and complicity, the labour movement and left have allowed the new right to claim the moral high ground in community care. If we are to evict them from this position, we must do more than merely show that their intentions are less than honourable, and that the likely effects of the reforms will be damaging – both of which are true. We must also re-establish the legitimacy of the labour movement and left by admitting the errors of the past, and acknowledge what is progressive about the reforms, before moving on to construct a genuinely radical left alternative. This is the logic behind the ordering of chapters within this book.

Within this context, and without making excuses for ourselves, we can say that legitimacy is only one reason why the community care reforms have not been more controversial. The labour movement and the left can claim some credit for some of the progressive features of the reforms. In particular the emphasis on planning for need and emphasis on social rights to care represented a partial retreat from pure Thatcherite principles in the face of a broad alliance of oppositional interests, of which public service unions formed a part. But lest this be cause for premature celebration I suggest that this has led to an attempt to realise the new right agenda by more devious means which, at least as far as community care reform is concerned, appears to have been partially successful. Close examination of the reforms show that while any rights to community care are only vaguely defined, there are very powerful mechanisms to ensure rationing by tight budgetary controls, and to push through extensive privatisation.

The reforms made local government the central agency responsible for community care. Local government has been so battered and politically weakened by Thatcherism and was so pleased and indeed surprised to be asked to do the job, that it has been reluctant to rock the boat, in case the government changed its mind. In the NHS the historical lack of priority given to care, and unabating cost pressures, have led professionals and managers to concentrate increasingly on acute work. With the notable exception of psychiatrists, they have not resisted the wholesale transfer of care, initially local government, but largely en route to the commercial, voluntary and 'informal' sectors of welfare. However, the contribution of the NHS to care is being cut much more rapidly and extensively than the community is being equipped to deal with it. The Labour front bench prior to the 1992 election developed proposals to strengthen the more progressive features of the 1990 reforms, for example through its pledge to appoint a Minister for Community Care. However within the election campaign itself community care hardly featured and there was a concentration

**8**

*Normality is
hard work*

upon the effects of privatisation and the health reforms on acute health care. In this way Labour helped to reinforce an acute bias, and failed to significantly challenge the Tories' approach to community care reform.

Yet though the community care reforms claim to be a smart new suit of clothes, they are largely a fig leaf for Tory policies of rationalisation and privatisation, which in practice will deepen rather than alleviate the existing bias against care in the welfare state. Social services departments are perceived as dealing with crisis help to marginalised social groups rather than a universal service (Baldock, 1989); a tendency which can only be exacerbated by the financial crisis now afflicting local government (Social Services Policy Forum, 1992). It is easy to see why the government favours the approach embodied in the reforms. The concentration of central government responsibility upon people who are acutely ill can be justified as more 'socially productive' investment in the employed or socially active population. Community care by contrast is more often concerned with what is regarded as socially 'unproductive' maintenance of the non-employed population, the numbers of whom are perceived as growing at an alarming rate, especially with an increasingly 'ageing' population.

This bias against care is not, however, just something perpetuated by the state and professional groups at the behest of the system as a whole: it also has deep roots in the consciousness of many ordinary people. The sad truth is that so far community care has not mattered sufficiently as an issue on which people will judge the overall record of governments. More people are likely to feel personally at risk if there are waiting lists for cancer operations, than if home helps or community nurses are not available. The former are more likely to be viewed as priority issues affecting a majority of 'us', while the latter are more often regarded as more peripheral problems affecting a minority of socially marginalised 'them'. Thus as well as constructing a more effective user-worker alliance, there is a need to get the message across that community care is a majority not a minority issue. This in turn means working hard to overcome a highly influential ideology and system of oppression which it is appropriate to call 'healthism'. Although its influence can to a considerable extent be attributed to the workings of the economic system, often assisted by the state and powerful professional groups, it also influences the attitudes and responses of many ordinary people, including trade unionists and people on the left.

## Healthism and Community Care

Healthism is an influential ideology and set of practices which polarise health on the one hand and sickness or disability on the other into normal/desirable and abnormal/undesirable states, as a basis for treating those who are seen as living on one or other side of this divide as either normal and valued, or abnormal and devalued people. Healthism as Robert Crawford (1980) has pointed out, both idealises the state of 'perfect health'

and makes it a goal to be attained by individual effort. Hence failure is blamed on the individual rather than society. A partial exception is made within healthism for those who are temporarily ill, if it is presumed that they will get or can be made better. Thus sickness happens to people who are otherwise healthy when it is temporary, and defines them when it is permanent. We temporarily catch a cold, have a nervous breakdown or a broken leg, but we become schizophrenics, epileptics and cripples if we do not make a full recovery. In Erving Goffman's memorable phrase, permanent sickness or disability leads to stigma and 'spoiled identities' (Goffman, 1964).

I show in this book how healthism has been and continues to be deeply embedded in state health and welfare services, though its forms have changed over time. People with long term sickness and disability have been expected to conform to the norms of the wider society, though these norms have changed over time, and so have the expected means of adjustment. My key arguments, which are crucial if community care is to be transformed into a majority issue by combating healthism, are that:

- the different forms of oppression affecting groups of sick or disabled people, though having specific features, are all manifestations of healthism;
- there are links, often hidden, between the oppression associated with healthism and the structures of power associated with class, gender, 'race' and other forms of social inequality;
- the line between health and sickness, normality and abnormality is a mythical one and does not exist in practice. We are all users or potential users of community care and 'perfect' health is a goal that few attain, though one to which we are increasingly expected to aspire;
- the same structures of power and inequality that are implicated in sickness and disability (Townsend, Davidson and Whitehead, 1988), also oppress workers in the health and caring services. These inequalities are widening in society as a result of government policies over the last 14 years, and the impact of the NHS and community care reforms on employed workers will widen them yet further.

Sections of the book chart the general effects of healthism historically from the early days of the industrial revolution to the end of the 1970s, and also follow the analysis through for three of the major groups of people who are currently being affected by the community care reforms – users of mental health services, people with learning difficulties, and older people. During the period of early industrialisation there was an expectation that some, like older people, would live in the community or, like 'lunatics', be admitted to asylums which would quickly and cheaply refashion and return them to normal society. However, as social divisions hardened with the completion of the industrialisation process, a much more pessimistic and disciplinary approach set in which led increasingly to exclusion of the 'unfit' in custodial institutions.

The coming of the welfare state in 1945, I argue, was associated with a renewed emphasis on optimism and universal social rights, but this was increasingly overshadowed by professionally dominated 'therapeutic' approaches which sought to change devalued people to fit into the wider 'healthist' society. I call these approaches to community care 'integrationist'. They removed the responsibility of society itself to change, while putting a progressive gloss on the policy of community care. In any case the increasing demands on state expenditure meant that this programme of care in the community was only partly and patchily funded, largely because in healthist terms it was of a lower social priority than services for the acutely ill, and a time of growing fiscal pressures on public expenditure.

The first part of the book shows how institutional bias played a central role in the social construction of dependency, but shows that this happened in a wider social and political context. It is not enough to blame the institutions, though they often exacerbated the problem. The implication of this analysis is that simply removing this form of dependency will not automatically allow people to stand on their own two feet, unless both continuing vulnerability is acknowledged and the wider social and economic causes of dependency are addressed. None of this however should be used as an excuse for slowing down the closure of indefensible institutions. As Nancy Korman and Howard Glennester (1985, p. 130) put it in their study of the Darenth Park Hospital closure programme in the 1980s:

> Twenty five years of community care policies with slow development of community care services, shows that the compromise of natural and gradual reduction of hospital places paralleled by community services does not work. Community services are being developed because the hospital is closing.

## Consumerism and the Alternatives

Through their emphasis on choice and user-involvement the 1990 reforms potentially open up a much more radical approach to community care, if we can free them of the new right ideology which constrains them.

The second half of the book, therefore, examines the processes of community care reform in the 1980s leading up to the 1990 NHS and Community Care Act, finding that though promising a new deal for previously devalued people, in practice this is only being delivered to a very limited degree. While appearing to respond to demands for social rights to individually sensitive services to be extended to devalued people, the familiar bias towards care will be maintained and even intensified in an increasing emphasis on privatisation, rationing, and informal care by the community. Chapter 5 charts how public services unions themselves have been seeking to respond to the 'new' community care.

Although the managerial-consumerist model embodied in the 1990 reforms might seem superficially attractive, it has many hidden snags which limit its use as a genuinely empowering strategy for progressive community care:

- it is wholly individualist, deflecting attention away from the need also for collective empowerment, and from the influence of 'race', gender and class inequalities on sickness and disability;
- it sees care as a 'product' to be delivered in pre-defined 'packages' in ways that will encourage the expert role to be assumed, as before, if not by professionals then by managers, devaluing or ignoring the expertise of users – and also because the need to ration will require the repression of genuine user choice;
- it perpetuates a divisive analytical distinction between consumer and producer, or user and worker that is not a satisfactory basis for a progressive community care which acknowledges the contribution of all participants to care. (Stacey, 1976)

Thus this book argues that a radical empowering approach to community care must overcome the managerialist/consumerist model and see all those involved in it as active producers of care, with different types of expertise to contribute, whether as employed professionals or care staff, volunteers, informal carers, or the 'users' of services themselves. Unless convincing arguments to the contrary can be put in particular instances, users need to be seen as the best judges of whether and in what ways they wish to complement their own expertise with resort to professional help. As my title suggests, 'normality is hard work' which can be performed by a range of people whom Abram de Swaan's quotation leaves deliberately ambiguous. By calling normality 'work' in this way, he:

- acknowledges the contributions made by all involved, which is consistent with the notion of community care as a democratic encounter between all producers;
- implies that it is hard work for everybody if to different degrees, in ways that should make us stop categorising users of community care as a social 'out group';
- recognises that normality or 'normal living' has to be worked at as something which is socially made, and hence might be chosen but also rejected, which is consistent with maximising user autonomy and choice;
- stresses that notions of normality themselves and the expectation that people should conform to them, are themselves capable of political

challenge and change.

This approach contrasts with the consensual and 'integrationist' notion of 'normal living' implicit in the 1990 reforms, which assume that community care can simply happen without major change in the wider society, and takes no account of the corrosive effects that more than a decade of Conservative economic and social policies have had on community life.

However it also departs significantly from the dominant approach to community care followed in the period 1945 to 1979. This involved professional dominance of need, similarly influenced by an integrationist discourse, which sought to 'fit' disabled people into the wider society. This involved, it is true, a greater recognition than subsequently of the need and right to receive a range of publicly provided services to make this possible, even if it was more promised than provided. The approach taken in this book therefore challenges both previous models by adopting a political rather than purely integrationist perspective on disability, which has emerged from radical sociology and user movements. It sees the wider culture as oppressive to people with disabilities and the shift to community care will therefore also necessitate challenging and changing healthist assumptions, institutions and practices.

The final section of the book therefore seeks to consider the practical implications of this critique. Chapter 6 outlines some alternative principles for good community care which seek to transcend the limitations of both the managerialist-consumerist model of the 1990 reforms and the professionally dominant model which preceded it. I argue for a democratisation of services to achieve a genuine 'pluralism' which balances the needs and interests of all producers while putting those of users at the forefront, to achieve 'user-centred and worker friendly' community care. These need to be both sensitive to individual need, and address the need for collective empowerment through radical social and economic change. I conclude by briefly asking how UNISON and the trade union movement can take forward the campaign for user centred and worker friendly community care, in the wider context of the struggle to defend, restore and democratise the public services.

# Chapter 1
# Institutional solutions and the prehistory of community care

## A Historical Perspective on Community Care

Recent developments in community care policies, particularly since the 1980s, cannot be understood without some account of the political-economic background from which they emerged. It is now clear that since the end of the 1970s there has been both a renewed impetus towards and a change in the emphasis of community care policies, dubbed by Alan Walker as 'the new politics of community care' which

> departed significantly from the, albeit weak, consensus that had existed
> in the previous forty years. Thus the emphasis has shifted away from care
> in the community by local authority personnel towards an even more
> confusing mixture of care by the community itself and private care, re-
> gardless of whether in domiciliary or institutional settings. (Walker, 1989,
> p.207)

How we assess the significance of this change, consolidated by the 1990 NHS and Community Care Act, depends on the ideological perspective it is viewed from. From a new right viewpoint it would of course be welcomed, a return of communal responsibility and choice, taken away by decades of state and professional monopolists and empire-builders. From a more centre-left position, it might more likely be represented as a weakening commitment to social justice, in response to growing cost and demographic pressures. A radical left position, such as began to be developed in the introduction to this book, might share many of the centre-left concerns about the implications of the reforms, but also those of the right about what went before. Since each of these stereotyped viewpoints, in looking at the present, makes historical assumptions about community care in the past, we need to ground our understanding of the new politics of community care in an evaluation of what preceded it. We need to decide which particular viewpoint has truth on its side.

Such a historical perspective on community care has a number of issues to sort out. It needs to explain why certain things happened when they did, particularly why community care policies of a particular kind began to emerge in the 1950s, why they were only patchily implemented in the 1960s and 1970s, and why the emphasis changed again in the 1980s. The value of history, however, lies not just in helping to explain why certain things happened, but also in alerting us to a wider set of political possibilities by identifying what did not but might have happened. With this in mind, we will examine two further issues. First, why community care didn't occur until the 1950s. Putting it another way, how did the institutional approach to community care originate and why did it persist for so long? To some extent, then, we have to examine the prehistory of community care, which was also the period in which institutionally-based public service unionism emerged.

The second issue is of more direct contemporary concern and reverberates through the remainder of this book. Though neither of the two dominant models of community care approximates to a 'user-centred and worker-friendly' approach in rhetoric at least, it is hard to escape the conclusion that the Conservatives' approach of the 1980s appears to take the issue of user empowerment more seriously. Thus from the perspective adopted by this book, one can not simply take sides with the earlier against the later version. The earlier version made a paper commitment for public provision of care in the community, but never made the resources available from central level to make it a reality or sought to empower users. The later version was much more preoccupied with cost containment, and advocated care by the community, but it also spoke the language of individual sensitivity to need and user empowerment, issues on which the earlier professionally-dominated version was strangely silent.

## Approaches to history: conservative, conventional and critical
Conservative advocates of community care often envisage a previous golden age before the welfare state, when Victorian values reigned supreme, and families looked after their own. A state of affairs corrupted by the welfare state, which it is presumed, brought about a decay in such responsibilities as people abandoned their dependent relatives to the state. Such a historical vision is one influence behind the 'new politics' of community care. However it was not a view invented by the new right, but rather one they successfully manipulated. Robert Moroney found it was a common view among civil servants and public decision makers in the early 1970s (Moroney, 1976). Careful historical analysis has, however, indicated that there is no factual foundation for the view that there has been a general increase in resort to institutional care in the 20th Century during the period of the rise of the welfare state (Dalley, 1988). Indeed Victorian values and the resort to institutionalisation of care went hand in hand, and the shift to community care is more a product of the welfare state.

## Comparing 'Conventional' and 'Critical' Approaches to the History of Institutions

**'Conventional'**

- Impetus to create institutions initially progressive
- Emphasis on ideas and values as influences on social reform
- Change initiated by humanitarian reformers, enlightened professionals and concerned pressure groups
- Evolutionary and incremental change leads (more or less) to gradual but steady progress
- State and professional intervention is generally beneficial and its effects gradually improve

**'Critical'**

- Institutions have controlling intentions and effects from the outset
- Emphasis on structural and economic influences on social reform
- Change occurs because activities of reformers are consistent with changing interests of dominant social groups
- Change not always unmitigated progress, but may also represent shifts in social control strategies by dominant groups, faced with challenge from below
- State and professional intervention is originally and remains often class, 'race' or gender biased

*Note:* these are of course only tendencies, and do not take into account internal diversity within different approaches, for example between feminist and Marxist influenced 'critical' approaches

Since the new right historical approach cannot help us, what are the alternatives? Conventional social administration has on the whole seen no contradiction between the emergence of an institutional approach to social problems at the beginning of the 19th Century, and the later development of community care. Within an evolutionary and reformist approach, both tend to be seen as stages on the road to progress, the one giving way naturally to the other. A classic example of this 'evolutionary' approach is Kathleen Jones' influential account of the development of the mental health services up to the early 1970s. The development of the lunatic asylums is seen, at least in the initial stages, as both a rational and humanitarian inspired attempt by enlightened reformers, state administrators and civil servants, working in harness with a rising body of state professionals, including doctors and nurses, to help people with an objectively definable set of problems. Although 'public opinion' sometimes hampered these efforts, by imposing financial constraints and custodial objectives on institutions, this climate of opinion changed with the coming of the welfare state after the Second World War, which enabled the early progressive potential to be better accomplished through policies such as community care (Jones, 1972).

This historical approach has been increasingly challenged by more critical perspectives which recognise that asylums and other institutions had controlling intentions and effects, even during their formative and supposedly more 'progressive' phase. In various ways, critical approaches see the creation of 'total institutions' by the state as dictated by the changing problems of social order created by industrial capitalism. They see professionals as not necessarily motivated by humanitarian concerns but also as 'moral entrepreneurs' ambitious for money, influence and power. They see the alliance between the state and professions such as medicine as creating the basis for the state to mask its social control intentions and represent these in benevolent and humanitarian terms. Within this critical consensus, of course, there is a considerable diversity of theoretical viewpoints, and while some critics see such total institutions as mostly disciplinary and controlling, others are more prepared to concede that some good was intended and done (for example, compare the approaches to 19th Century lunacy reform taken by Andrew Scull, 1979 and Vieda Skultans, 1979, Ch 7).

Critical perspectives also emphasise that the resort to institutional solutions can only be understood in the context of the changing patterns of state welfare as a whole, and how this was linked to wider social and economic transformations. This involved not only different ways of dealing with familiar social problems, but the redefinition of social problems in the light of newly emerging norms of social behaviour, associated with the rise of industrial capitalism.

## Disability and Industrial Capitalism

The development of industrial capitalism involved a move away from communal and more co-operative patterns of work and living, a so-called 'moral economy', to a more individualist ideology and way of life, associated with the spreading factory and wage system and urban living. The newly emergent system, based on separation of work from home and family from community, placed a premium on the ability to perform market labour – to travel to and from work, to work continuously for long hours day after day, and at a pace increasingly dictated by mechanised production. Disability became defined in terms of these increasingly stringent social requirements of waged labour under industrial capitalism. In this sense it was socially created by them, as the previous system of production and social organisation meant disability was likely to be less socially visible (Oliver, 1990; Barnes 1992, Ch 2).

The Victorian system of state welfare was one which sought to refine fur-

The 1601 Elizabethan Poor Law is sometimes contrasted with the more punitive and harsh approach taken by the Victorian Poor Law after 1834. These contrasts can be too sharply drawn, however. The 1601 Act was quite often harsh in its effects, sought to impose responsibility for welfare and care on families, and pioneered forms of institutional confinement consistent with the spreading market economy, which were to become only too widespread under the Victorian system.

This is the famous poetical account of the typical mixed workhouse penned by George Crabbe towards the end of the eighteenth century:

> There Children dwell who know no parents' care;
> Parents, who know no children's love, dwell there;
> Heart-broken Matrons on their joyless bed,
> Forsaken Wives and Mothers never wed;
> Dejected Widows with unheeded tears,
> And crippled Age with more than childhood's fears;
> The Lame, the Blind, and, far the happiest they!
> The moping Idiot and the Madman gay.

Quoted by Raymond Williams, *The Country and the City*, p 108

**18**

*Normality is
hard work*

ther the emerging systems of categorising and controlling forms of disability more closely. The normal social expectations of 'competitive individualism' were established through the 1834 Poor Law, and its linchpin the workhouse system, which placed an obligation on every adult male and able-bodied labourer to work to maintain himself and his dependants on a wage. At the time this was a relatively new principle, and there was considerable resistance to the idea from large sections of the working class who thought their 'birthright' to relief had been removed. On the whole labour was scarce, and industry expanding, so the state's aim was to encourage entry into the labour force at the available wage rates, under the threat of removal to the workhouse. Previous rights to various forms of relief in the community under the 'allowance system' were expressly taken away by the 1834 Act (Thompson, 1963; Fraser, 1986).

At the same time the new system of poor relief established what Deborah Stone calls certain 'categorical exemptions from the labour market' (Stone, 1984). In theory these applied to youth, widowhood, and old age, as well as sickness and disability, by which means boundaries were drawn between the 'deserving' and the 'undeserving' poor, or as she puts it, between a 'work' and a 'needs-based' distributive system. The aim of this distinction, she argues, was to ensure the primacy of the work-based system in order to reinforce the work ethic, by restricting access to 'privileged' treatment to a limited number of definable groups. This distinction needed to be carefully policed to prevent faking, and this is where doctors became increasingly important, as 'neutral' experts and gatekeepers to such preferential treatment. As Stone recognises, however, a theoretical right to privileged status from the state did not necessarily mean it was granted in practice. Many – probably the majority – struggled on without public assistance, relying on what family and community support could be mustered, but often leading as Oliver (1990) puts it, to segregation *within* the community. Those entering the workhouse system were often not granted privileges, or only to a limited and grudging degree. The long term sick were entitled to home treatment and an allowance, but usually only if they could prove inability to work. So-called 'defectives' – initially the blind, deaf, dumb and later the physically disabled – were entitled to similar treatment. The old and infirm were in theory entitled to an 'outdoor' allowance, or special privileges in the workhouse, but did not always receive them for fear that this might discourage people from saving for old age or caring for relatives (Townsend, 1962; Hodgkinson, 1967; Fraser, 1974; Stone, 1984). Troublesome or 'refractory' lunatics were removed to asylums, but Poor Law authorities were reluctant to transfer compliant 'cases' because asylum care, though very basic, was typically more expensive than maintenance in the workhouse (Scull, 1979).

That privileged treatment for certain categories of people became more usual from the 1870s onwards had more to do with a determination to reassert the harsh principles of 'less eligibility' for the able bodied, than any humanitarian intent. At the same time as efforts were made to sort the able from the non able-bodied, increasing emphasis was placed on differentiating among the different classes of disabled people. In Michael Rose's 'conventional' or evolutionary perspective, this is seen as early signs of a more progressive approach, a recognition of varieties of need, and the development of professional expertise around them, that would ultimately lead to a welfare state (Rose, 1972). An alternative, more critical explanation is that as well as making it easier to justify a tougher approach to the able-bodied, it also made it possible to differentiate among the non able-bodied, in order to determine who could potentially be returned to capitalist society and its 'work-based system of distribution'.

## Separating the Pauper Host

Thus institutions were set up not just to maintain but also to categorise and separate out elements of the non able-bodied pauper host who might, in differing ways and to differing degrees, be deemed appropriate for 'resocialisation'. The processes by which this happened were highly complex, but some broad general trends can be identified. First a particular group

with a particular set of needs was identified. Second, separate and experimental forms of provision were pioneered, often out of a philanthropic impulse, and a high degree of success claimed for them. Third, a social reform movement was initiated to make such supposedly beneficial institutions more generally available through the state. Fourth, occupational and professional movements emerged claiming specialist expertise in the systems of social classification and technologies of resocialisation. Of these, the rising medical profession sought, and eventually in most cases obtained, the dominant position within each institutional order, and this itself was one of the most important influences upon the growing tendency towards medical specialisation. In some instances, particularly lunacy reform, scandals associated with private enterprise provision spurred state action (Parry-Jones, 1972).

These processes were part of a more general faith in institutional solutions to social problems which was characteristic of the early Victorian era. It is now more generally recognised that these played a crucial part in easing the transition from a tradition-bound and communal-based, localist social order to one based on principles of mobility, social competence and individual competitiveness in a market economy (Rothman, 1971; Foucault, 1977; Ignatieff, 1983). Reformed institutions of almost infinite variety, including schools, workhouses, prisons, hospitals, asylums, and reformatories, were set up to help inculcate the individualistic values and appropriate forms of behaviour of the emerging society, and to deal with its casualties. Such institutions were represented as organised on both uniquely modern and more humane, as well as more socially efficient principles than the often barbarous prisons, Bridewells and Bedlams of the past. However, though this point may well be conceded, this should not deceive us (as it did conventional historians of social administration) about the fundamentally disciplinary intent of such institutions, which devised more subtle, effective and pervasive technologies of social control than in the past, and applied them to far greater numbers of people (Foucault, 1977).

When seen in this light, there is less of a contradiction between the laissez-faire and non-interventionist values of the Victorian state, on the one hand, and its massive public investment in such institutions on the other. The attitudes necessary to make an individualistic, laissez-faire society work required massive state intervention to complement the disciplinary effects of the spreading competitive labour market and factory system. According to Fiona Williams (1989a) though the nature and effects of state intervention varied, it was constrained by forms of social discipline and norms of behaviour associated not just with the core institutions of work, but also family and nation; with social divisions of gender and 'race', as well as class. Professions and institutions played a crucial role in categorising people as socially 'fit' or 'unfit' in relation to these requirements, and in then devising technologies to change people or minimise their perceived disruptive effects.

One of the most important socially-created categories, one that often proved just as difficult to sustain in practice then as now, was defining people according to whether their prime disability was either mental or physical. Once this line was drawn, further categorisations were then made, often in order to assess the potential for social rehabilitation, between those people deemed to have acute or chronic disabilities. It should not be assumed that these labels were easily stuck on different groups of people. We know that intense struggles were often fought around them between professions and state officials, and also within professions such as medicine. We know much less about the degree of resistance offered by those at the receiving end of the labelling process, although this is starting to emerge out of oral history research and autobiographical accounts. Professions such as medicine had what some have described as an 'imperialist' interest in expanding their potential or actual clientele, and in emphasising the therapeutic possibilities of intervention.

## Establishing the Liberal-Professional Model

The outcomes of this process varied enormously in different sectors, in terms of whether a 'liberal professional' model became established. Within its framework a lay person is expected at an appropriate point to seek professional help for some problem, but is under no legal compulsion to do so. However, having once entered the encounter, he or she is expected to submit to the expertise and 'reasonable' authority of the professional, until the problem is judged to have been cured (Parsons, 1951). Under this model, the role of the state is limited on the one hand by a rule of non-interference in matters which are a matter of professional expertise, and on the other by the need to protect the voluntary nature of professional-client encounters. The state can provide the resources, but cannot dictate what happens once the doctor has convinced the state that this model is appropriate.

Acute medicine and surgery succeeded in establishing such a model based largely on claims to diagnostic and therapeutic competence. This enabled it, prior to the current NHS reforms, largely to free itself of external controls within the context of state funded services, as therapeutic optimism grew in leaps and bounds. In the three case studies examined here – mental health services, services for people with learning difficulties, and services for older people – the situation was rather different. In the first two the initial therapeutic optimism concerning social rehabilitation soon dissipated, and medical autonomy within the state was only partially established. Doctors' ability to judge people mad or sane, mentally competent or mentally deficient was only partially accepted, within a system that increasingly became custodial rather than curative. Consequently, the courts and the police still played a significant role in initiating and regulating professional encounters (Busfield, 1986). Although the liberal-professional model may have formally been established in services for older people, this was not associated with any degree of therapeutic optimism, and in practice its conditions were often breached as associations of old age with senility and lack of social competence often led to imposed treatment.

As a result, there was a sea change in the social function of the institutions established for each of these three socially defined groups. The three principles of institutional provision identified for the non able-bodied – privileged status, rehabilitation, and exclusion and containment — are not mutually exclusive. However there was without doubt a progressive shift away from the first two and towards the third, which has been well documented in each instance (for example, for lunatic asylums see Scull, 1979; Busfield, 1986; for services for people with learning difficulties see Ryan and Thomas, 1980; for older people Townsend, 1962).

## From Covert to Overt Social Control

Within critical sociological perspectives, even the liberal-professional model is often seen as a form of covert social control, rather than a wholly neutral form of help. We hear an inner voice telling us we must seek the right kind of help, and co-operate with professionals' determined attempts to make us better. We think we are choosing to do this, but in reality we have been socialised into it by our nearest and dearest, as well as the wider culture (as suggested, in their different ways, by Parsons, 1951; Freidson, 1970 and Foucault, 1973). If we stopped to think, we might ask more critical questions or seek alternatives.

In the three sectors which we are examining here, however, services shifted increasingly from covert to more overt forms of social control, and the reasons why this should be so are hotly disputed between conventional and critical approaches.

Traditionally this shift has been attributed to stigmatising social attitudes towards, and the resulting discrimination suffered by, devalued social groups. More sociological explanations seek to explain the social context in which this occurred, and how it was reinforced by economic and political structures. While we should be careful not to attribute every negative effect to industrial capitalism, or to draw too rosy a picture of disability in pre-capitalist society, there is little doubt that the premium placed on being able-bodied helped to emphasise and reinforce the stigma and disadvantages of disability. Above all, even when accorded 'privileged status' people with disabilities were still defined as a problem, not the society which (for example through industrial accidents) was often responsible for causing the disability, and which was organised in such a way as to make 'ordinary living' extremely difficult for people with disabilities. However in the early days of industrialisation, when the economy was expanding, there was considerable 'therapeutic optimism' that institutional treatment would in many cases lead to rapid reintegration into a buoyant labour market.

This individualising effect of policies led to a focus on people with disabilities in ways which therefore also often facilitated the shift from covert to more overt forms of social control, based on the widely held view that they were a burden or even a threat to society. This discourse, though fitting in with the needs of the most powerful groups in society, also struck a chord with many working class families struggling to cope with caring responsibilities in precarious economic circumstances, and helped to legitimise institutional care among working class people (Scull, 1979; Crowther, 1981; Ignatieff, 1983).

Though a detailed historical analysis would be necessary in each instance, some common features were associated with services which shifted increasingly to overt social control:

- from the outset there was an underlying emphasis on order and discipline in institutional routines, which leant itself to more overt forms of discipline;
- concerns to minimise cost in the face of rising institutional populations led to spartan conditions and staffing ratios which heightened the disciplinary approach and frustrated rehabilitation;
- a restrictive Poor Law system encouraged social segregation of groups who could not easily be integrated into the labour market.

A more controversial issue is the influence of growing medicalisation upon institutional routines. Within a conventional evolutionary perspective it is external interference which prevented the emergence of a treatment-focused, liberal professional model. For example Jones (1972) argues that the development of mental health services was held back by the legalistic requirements of the 1890 Lunacy Act. Only when doctors were freed from this by the 1959 Mental Health Act could a more therapeutic and liberal approach develop, consistent with an emphasis on community care. Others have argued, however, that medical control of institutions was quite consistent with a pessimistic and stigmatising approach which helped to sanction social exclusion in the patient's and society's interest, and justified subsequent close supervision by doctors and nurses or other care staff (for example, see Scull (1979) for mental health services, Oliver (1990) for people with physical disabilities, Ryan and Thomas (1980) for people with learning difficulties, and Fennell, Phillipson and Evers (1988, Ch 8) for older people in institutional care). Thus critical approaches to the history of institutions emphasise the role of doctors' own 'therapeutic pessimism' in reinforcing these wider social processes.

## Eugenics and Therapeutic Pessimism

This growing pessimism in theory and practice was strongly reinforced at the end of the 19th Century by the increasing influence of eugenics on both the state and the medical profession. The pseudo-science of eugenics was developed by Francis Galton, and adapted Darwinian principles to the study of medical and social problems. Differences between societies and social groups within them were explained biologically. Eugenics gave support to state action to ameliorate social conditions where this could be said to have a positive physical effect in improving 'national efficiency', such as the provision of school meals for needy children. It also placed considerable emphasis on the supposed hereditary causes of disease and social problems, favouring selective breeding to improve the national 'stock'. This in turn created an alliance between the medical profession and the state to exclude the so-called unfit (Jones, 1986). The influence of eugenics can be clearly seen in the highly restrictive principles of the 1890 Lunatics Act, which emphasised certification and permanent exclusion of 'lunatics'. It was an even more prominent influence on the 1913 Mental Deficiency Act which served to medicalise the exclusion and control of large numbers of working class men and women, many with only very mild learning difficulties (Ryan and Thomas, 1980; Williams and Walmsley, 1990, Part Two).

The emergence of eugenics was linked to wider political and economic shifts occurring in British society at the end of the 19th Century. Thus biological notions of fitness justified state intervention abroad to impose an empire on supposedly inferior Africans and Asians, and at home to improve environmental conditions for working class people on the grounds of social efficiency. Since eugenic principles explicitly favoured a more collectivist approach by the state, they were often endorsed by Fabian socialists such as Sidney and Beatrice Webb. Changing economic circumstances also favoured exclusion and custodial approaches. There was a shift to larger scale factory production which favoured an adaptable workforce, with both a reasonably developed basic education and degree of physical fitness. The unemployment associated with the Great Depression of the 1870s-90s, and 1920s and 1930s increased the visibility of people with disabilities. These circumstances, as Stone (1984) suggests, encouraged governments to see larger numbers of people as ineligible for work and social participation and subject either to conditional exemption in the community or exclusion in institutions.

Precisely how such ideological and economic influences exerted an influence varied in each instance. For older people, the emergence of retirement from the early 20th Century onwards is seen as crucial by many critical writers to the 'social construction of dependency' in old age, under the guise of creating a privileged condition. Thus, state pensions, originating in 1908, and universalised on a contributory basis in 1925 during the depression years, and the emergence of geriatrics as a medical specialty defining old age as a separate state with separate medical needs, are some of the developments that can plausibly be traced back to these political and economic origins (see Estes, 1979; Roebuck, 1979; Walker, 1983; Fennell, Phillipson and Evers, 1988).

For people with learning difficulties, it is clear that the emergence of childhood as a separate sphere (Aries, 1962) in the wake of the political and economic changes associated with the industrial revolution, was one fundamentally important background influence. The associated exclusion of children from productive labour, though often represented as unmitigated progress influenced entirely by humanitarian concerns, occurred also in the context of the technological and economic changes described above (just as has the increasing prolongation of childhood and adolescence since the end of the Second World War). However what intensified the pressure for increased state intervention in the lives of people with learning difficulties was, in the first instance, the spread of universal state primary education after 1870. Experts and authorities wanted to find ways of distinguishing between those working class children who could benefit from state education, and thus make a future contribution to the industrial economy, and those for whom it was deemed wasted expenditure. The evolution of supposedly scientific intelligence testing was heavily influenced by such considerations.

On top of this, however, was the political pressure generated by middle class moral panics about working class sexual mores, delinquent behaviour and general disorderliness. Middle class fears of 'swamping' by unfit members of the working class underpinned the legal and medical categorisation and sanctioned the exclusion of many unmarried teenage mothers as 'defective', and their children being taken away from them. For boys, petty crime was a more usual route to the asylum than sexual activity; it being suggested that they were often led astray by 'clever' criminals (Ryan and Thomas 1980, Ch 5; Tyne, 1982; Soder, 1984). Up to the 1940s, other countries took this philosophy further towards its logical conclusion, from the forced sterilisation undertaken in many parts of the USA, to the mass murder of Nazi concentration camps. In Britain, exclusion in 'colonies', where 'mental defectives' could 'be themselves', was represented as a humane solution, but it occurred within a repressive consensus that people so defined were a potential or actual social threat.

Only a minority of those officially deemed mentally defective were incarcerated in asylums. The state was torn in two directions, especially during the inter-war period of economic crisis. While on the one hand work scarcity favoured the expansion of numbers of people defined as disabled, on the other the associated state expenditure crisis held this tendency in check. The favoured solution was closely controlled supervision for the majority in the community, which has been rather too rosily represented by some writing from an evolutionary viewpoint as the origins of 'community care' (Jones, 1972).

Eugenicist notions defined particular groups as problems in ways that were often class-biased, sexist and racist. Thus it was not coincidental that in 1866 John Langdon Down categorised significant numbers of the inmates of asylums as 'Mongols', for he explicitly regarded them as racial 'throwbacks' (Fernando, 1991, p.41). Similarly the larger numbers of women than men in asylums was explained in terms of them being more biologically prone to mental disease, because they were at a lower stage of evolutionary development and not in control of their faculties (Showalter, 1987; Ussher, 1991). The lower reaches of the working class were regarded as peopled by degenerates who were similarly regarded as prone to mental disease and deficiency. Older people were defined as more like children and hence less capable and in need of supervision. The white upper class adult male was of course at the top of the evolutionary ladder and others ranged on steps below it, according to age, gender, class and 'racial group'. Eugenicist views of particular 'problem groups' were thus part of a more comprehensive world view of superiority, inferiority, and social dominance.

Page margin number

## Policing the 'Underclass'

Specific policy developments towards defined groups of people have com-

mon threads which link them to much wider political and economic developments, including the spread of a more collectivist ideology, growing state intervention, and the growing political and economic dominance of western industrialised societies. Domestically they can be linked to the partial decay of the individualistic and residual Poor Law system, and the associated redrawing of the boundaries between the deserving and undeserving poor, which was referred to earlier in this chapter. From the end of the 19th Century, official policy increasingly distinguished between and sought different means of dealing with the respectable and less respectable elements of the working class. The former needed help through social insurance and other measures to prevent them falling into the condition of the latter, regarded as an underclass or 'residuum'. Members of the ruling orders were very preoccupied with fears about what might happen if a political alliance was forged between the two groups (Steadman Jones, 1971; Squires, 1990). As well as this threat from within, the British establishment was also worried about the threat to its economic and political position in the world posed by the rise of Germany and the USA.

The basic response to this situation was to extend social rights such as pensions and unemployment insurance to those defined as belonging to the former group of people. The latter however continued to be closely policed, less by the Poor Law, which was formally abolished after 1929, than by the more socially neutral seeming 'public assistance institutions', mental hospitals and mental defective colonies of the inter-war period. In reality these were simply a more socially sanitised means of parcelling up the policing of the different elements of the underclass. (The way that the notion of the underclass was originally constructed, and how it has resurfaced in different forms and applied to different contexts, including contemporary poverty, has been more fully charted by the social historian John Macnichol (1987).)

Of course, more detailed historical analysis would, to some extent, qualify this pessimistic assessment in particular instances. Thus as Andy Treacher and Geoff Baruch (1981) argue, the 1929 Labour government sought in a half-hearted way through the 1930 Mental Treatment Act to transform the mental health services along universalistic and treatment-focused lines. This led to some innovations, such as the possibility for the first time of voluntary treatment, and also some treatments of dubious value such as insulin shock therapy. In its wake there was also the development of some community care, such as outpatient services and 'after care'. However the Act was timid in conception, only nibbling away at the edges of the Victorian system, and in any case got squeezed by the expenditure crisis of the 1930s economic depression (see the illuminating contemporary account by Paul Winterton (1938)).

Thus, with the exception of acute general hospitals, the predominant social weight of public total institutions on the eve of the creation of the welfare state was towards policing the underclass in an age of mass unemployment. To provide too comfortable conditions in asylums, colonies or public assistance institutions was regarded as dangerous in circumstances where outside living conditions were so bad. It might encourage people or their relatives to feign need in order to get admission. Stories of unemployed people faking madness in the 1930s to gain admission to mental hospitals were common.

## Public Total Institutions as Places of Waged Labour

Before moving on to examine the emergence of community care in the 1950s, I want to try to bring a 'waged work' perspective to bear on the development of public total institutions, as places where working class people have made a livelihood. This is one of the most neglected aspects of the history of institutional care.

My starting point is Ignatieff's (1983) argument that the partial social acceptability of asylums was facilitated because they helped working class families deal with caring dilemmas. I would argue that this needs to be extended to include their growing importance as centres of working class employment. As a result such institutions came understandably to be defended by sections of the working class for whom they offered not only jobs, but also the basis around which to create a stable if often a geographically and socially isolated working class community life. Asylum employment, particularly in the rural areas where they were mainly established, also became one of the chief working class escape routes from low paid agricultural labour and domestic service (Carpenter, 1980). Later, in the interwar period, the route was widened to draw in people from the depressed areas of Britain; and in the 1950s and '60s from Eire and Commonwealth countries. This economic and social interest of public institution workers in the perpetuation of such places provides the basis for a potential alliance with other forces wishing to defend such institutions, including professional elites, and relatives of working class inmates who had been relieved of often onerous caring responsibilities.

If it is generally true, as Scull (1979) argues for 19th Century lunatic asylums, that the medical profession became an institutional elite by claiming expertise as society's 'moral entrepreneurs', much of the day-to-day custodial and stigmatising work was delegated to waged labourers, the mass of attendants and nurses who enjoyed few of the privileges accorded to their superiors. As pessimism set in and custodial regimes became entrenched, the work itself became defined as socially contaminating, and hence 'underclass' work, or, as it was put at the time, work by 'the unemployed of other classes'.

COHSE, perhaps to a greater extent than other public service unions, was the product of this custodial and institutional-based asylum and Poor Law system, and had an ambiguous relationship with it for much of its history. The initial response of the National Asylum Workers' Union (NAWU) when it was formed in 1910 was to seek to demystify the nature of the work. It rejected employer attempts to foist a 'professional attitude' upon rank-and-file workers. It argued uncompromisingly that the work was degrading, but sought 'fair' rewards and treatment from superiors. This position, which was enforced by militant strike action after the First World War did not challenge the fundamentally custodial nature of the system, only workers' treatment within it.

This outlook was subsequently modified, for two reasons. First, the high unemployment of the inter-war period weakened the earlier anti-employer, anti-psychiatrist stance. Second, employers realised that there might be gains made in coming to terms with trade unionism, and a stable alliance was forged between the medical elite, employing authorities and the union. As a result, the union increasingly adopted a more service-oriented, professional approach, in broad terms supportive of the treatment model under medical direction, established by the 1930 Mental Treatment Act.

For the most part the union's shift to professionalism was thus conservative. The ethos of the Mental Hospitals and Institutional Workers Union (MHIWU) became largely that of a 'loyal servant', supportive of employer and medical claims that gradual progress was being made in difficult economic circumstances to deal with mental illness, and helping to shield mental hospitals from public criticism. The major exception to this conservatism was the MHIWU's success in campaigning in the labour movement in the 1930s against the 'voluntary' sterilisation of people with learning difficulties, when many medical and employing authorities favoured it (Carpenter, 1988; Jones, 1986, p.102). This did not of itself necessarily question the need for their social exclusion. The union was in something of a quandary about this, because the expansion of the system was leading to growing employment in this sector, which was one of the factors behind the union's growth in membership in the 1930s.

The history of the Poor Law side of COHSE's history in the inter-war period is similar. There was little questioning of the need for the Poor Law system by either the Poor Law Workers' Trade Union (PLWTU) or its successor, the Poor Law Officers' Union (PLOU), which even initiated a campaign to save it in the 1920s (Carpenter, 1988). There was nothing inevitable about such defensive, if understandable, 'workerism'. After all, COHSE's predecessors did on occasion take wider moral stands beyond the immediate interests of their members, as the campaign against sterilisation shows.

# Chapter 2
# Community care in the
# 1950s and beyond

*Normality is
hard work*

This chapter, like the previous one, will provide a general account of policy developments within their wider political and economic context and
then examine how they affected users of mental health services, people with
learning disabilities, and older people. The main trends are clear. With the
creation of the welfare state after 1945 there was a pronounced if hesi-
tant and delayed shift to state and professionally run care *in* the community which gathered pace in the 1950s and 1960s. However rhetoric never
matched reality in provision, and the late 1970s began to see a growing emphasis upon informal care *by* the community, even before the Conservative
government came to power in 1979.

   The previous chapter challenged the conservative notion of a Victorian golden age in which families 'cared for their own', arguing instead
that the economic and ideological environment of the age encouraged an
institutional bias. It also challenged the 'conventional' approach to community care which sees the growth of medicalised institutions as paving the
way for it. In this chapter I try to show how community care, though it
contained many agendas, must be seen as primarily activated by the political
and economic changes associated with the shift to a welfare state based on
principles of universalism rather than selective help, and social inclusion
rather than exclusion. This came about partly as a result of popular pressure from below arising out of a war fought against fascism. It came also out
of a confidence that economic growth and full employment would finance
social programmes and draw marginalised groups into economic activity.
Such political economic changes were favourable to a shift away from the
stigmatising and controlling services of the past, part of which involved a
pronounced shift to the community.

## A New Form of 'Healthism'?
The previous system had been firmly based on principles of 'healthism',
which was defined in the Introduction as a dominant social ideology and
set of practices that defines health as a normal and desirable state, and

healthy people as normal and worthy people. Those who are deemed to lack these qualities for more than a temporary period may be perceived and treated as potential threats or burdens. If they cannot be quickly cured the most they can hope for, as Stone (1984) argued, is a form of closely supervised 'invalidity'. However, they will often find themselves physically excluded, a process sanctioned by the institutions set up from the Victorian period onwards, by the state and voluntary agencies, to 'help' such people.

The political changes associated with the war and welfare state offered the prospect of a challenge to this ideology, not least because the Nazi state had represented the extreme version of an 'institutional' solution informed by healthism. Such a challenge was mounted, but its impact became blunted largely because 'chronicity' was more optimistically redefined as acute illness within the biomedical model of health. Biomedical approaches, although optimistic about what can be achieved by curative technologies, often reinforce stigma where such illness can not be cured. They thus heighten the acute and curative bias. An example of healthism in this context is the tendency of health professionals to avoid patients whom they know to be dying (Sudnow, 1967). Healthism reinforces the tendency for priority to be given to younger, more acutely ill users. In the mental health services it led to the development of a two tier system in which the needs of people using acute units in general hospitals for short periods were prioritised, and those in the long stay hospitals accorded 'Cinderella' status (Busfield, 1986).

Rather than changing society's healthist notions of normality, there was thus a renewed therapeutic optimism which sought to remodel impaired individuals to make them fit for integration into the existing society. This was convenient for those benefiting from the existing power structure of society, and enhanced the reputation and standing of the professionals who claimed to be able to work such miracles. Community care therefore never fully challenged healthist assumptions. The wider society was only prepared to accept people back providing they had been modified, and it quickly became clear that the extent to which this could be achieved by drugs and technology had been exaggerated.

The 1990 community care reforms to a large extent accept that this curative model has been at best only partially successful and that, to varying degrees, there is a need to shift to a social rather than medical model of care in the community. On the face of it then, they offer a much more concerted assault on healthism. I will argue later that the reforms may in practice intensify the marginalisation and devaluation of caring services.

## Antecedents of Community Care

For whatever reasons, the shift to the community did not appear overnight. With more space, it would be possible to trace its historical antecedents in more detail. Some have already been mentioned, the fact that certain 'privileged' groups were sometimes allowed to receive support outside the workhouse, or that it was not feasible to incarcerate everyone. The most significant shift to the community however occurred from the 1870s when the Charity Organisation was set up to supervise assistance to the needy and deserving poor in their homes, with the express intention that the workhouse could then better and more strictly deal with the work shy and irretrievably degenerate. Philanthropic 'rescue work', aimed primarily at preventing 'decent' working people from sliding into and swelling the mass of the residuum, was thus an early indication of a shift to the community (Stedman Jones, 1971). Much of this attempt to 're-moralise' the poor offered advice and sometimes forms of assistance (such as housing) which were particularly aimed at women, and sought to enlist their support to create stable and self-reliant working class communities within the context of an urbanised market society (Wilson, 1977).

This initial shift to the community therefore represented a different form of social control, but one which also complemented institutional means of policing working class people. It could also be seen as more pervasive and interventionist; seeking to cross the working class threshold as a friend. There were many motives behind 19th Century philanthropy, and some were not necessarily noble (Fraser, 1986). Philanthropy not only helped to shore up a Poor Law system under challenge and creaking at the seams, but also sought to stabilise industrial and urban capitalism at a time when there were not only fears of growing disorder, but of the growing industrial and political assertiveness of organised labour. Philanthropy was in part an explicit attempt through 'social work' to heal the growing division between the classes through friendly personal contact, which would leave the poor feeling obliged to their betters (Stedman Jones, 1971). Even if many people were genuinely helped, there was a controlling sting in the tail. Although a concept devised and applied in the 1970s and 1980s, Philip Abrams's concept of 'colonisation' seems an apt description of what happened, especially when one considers that philanthropists like General Booth, founder of the Salvation Army, talked imperialistically in terms of 'darkest England'. Abrams defined colonisation of the community as that which:

> encompassed a range of relationships in which the neighbourhood was, in effect, either directly invaded by statutory or voluntary services or indirectly dominated by them. Either way, informal resources were tapped and bound to the purpose of the colonisers. A bridge was built but the traffic across it was almost entirely one way. (Bulmer, 1986, p.207)

Working class people largely saw the hidden agendas behind much philanthropy, and demanded something better.

It was this demand which set the context for much wider social reform.

In my day we didn't have social workers. We just had busybodies and do gooders and the bosom of the family — *eee* it were terrible.

For the first half of the 20th Century, the particular emphasis on community provision was on state social insurance. Though this established a right to assistance in unemployment, sickness and old age, free of the taint of the workhouse or philanthropy, and was partly financed by employers and the state, the right to benefit was conditional on establishing a contribution record. This excluded many – women, children, the long term unemployed – who were only brought into the system, if at all, on humiliating conditions, such as the hated 'means test' of the 1930s. As part of their price for fighting the Second World War, working class people demanded and won a shift to a more universal system of social protection, free of the stigma or humiliating conditions of the past.

Careful analysis of the post-Second World War reforms emanating from the Beveridge Report of 1942 shows that they did not offer the degree of social protection from the 'cradle to the grave' that was claimed for them (Ginsburg, 1979; Williams, 1989). As Peter Townsend puts it, they provided 'minimal rights for the many' rather than 'distributive justice for all'. Nevertheless they represented a very significant extension of social rights, within a climate emphasising entitlement to health and welfare services. This new climate was very much one of an upsurge in radicalism and an extension of democracy attendant on the defeat of fascism, and emphasis on social reconstruction, that brought the Labour Party to power on a landslide in 1945.

One of the consequences of this new political climate was a redefinition of the role of institutions. They now had to justify themselves as functionally necessary, in the growing anti-fascist and anti-authoritarian political culture. One of the earliest manifestations of this was Bowlby's work criticising the affects of institutions on childhood development. The 1948 Children's Act was one of the earliest products of this anti-institutional movement and shift to 'community care'. It is justifiable to see in this a partial move away from war-time collectivism, a plot to get women out of the factories and back into the home caring for children (Wilson, 1977). However, this should not obscure the inherent democratic impulse behind the anti-institutional movement.

I am not arguing that the radical emphasis on social rights and democracy was the only influence on the development of the welfare state. The example above shows that more conservative social and political elements were seeking to realise their objectives within its framework. Thus the welfare state was also influenced, as leading architects like Beveridge and Keynes made clear, by economic considerations. First, it was hoped that full employment and economic growth would ensure sufficient resources to finance the welfare state. Second, that state investment in health and welfare would itself be indirectly economically productive (Gough, 1979). It was also predicated in wider terms on the development of large scale mass production industry, which it was felt within a managed economy could provide work for all – a system which it is now usual to call Fordism (see Allen, 1992). The other major conservative influence on the welfare state was, to varying degrees, professionalism and bureaucracy. In the absence of any direct means of popular participation, people's access to their 'social rights' was to be mediated and thus controlled by bureaucrats or experts (Ginsburg, 1979; Addison, 1982). The overall effect of this was to heighten the more conservative pressures on the welfare state.

The initial shift to community care, implicit in its principles from the outset, was therefore influenced by the interplay between contradictory political and economic processes, the tension that existed between meeting both people's needs and those of the economic system. It was later to be shaped by what happened when these complacent economic assumptions ran into increasing trouble in the 1970s, as well as by the more concerted political challenge since the 1960s from both left and right, to bureaucracy and professionalism. Let us therefore look now at how these tensions were played out in particular instances, and with what results.

## Community Care in Mental Health Services

Community care was a delayed event, implicit in the community approach favoured within the welfare state on political and economic grounds. The shift was most prominent in the 1950s in the mental health services; the reasons for which have been hotly debated. Most sophisticated accounts, whether conventional or critical, are sceptical of the widely held 'technological' explanation – that the invention of new drugs like Largactil (Chlorpromazine) made it possible in the short run to treat and discharge people previously thought to be hopeless cases – and point to the wider social context in which the 'drugs revolution' occurred. Beyond this, however, the reasons are strongly contested, according to whether the needs of the social system or those of mental health service users are seen as most influential on developments.

For example, from a evolutionary perspective, Kathleen Jones (1973) argues that the drugs revolution was made possible by the emergence of a much more treatment-focused service. Doctors took a more professional approach, and this in turn was facilitated by absorption of the asylums into the National Health Service and the welfare state. As with general medicine, a network of linked professional services within the community and the hospital would now be provided, as appropriate. It would not be the asylum or nothing, which previously deterred people from seeking early treatment. The transformation of the patient-doctor relationship along liberal professional lines, with particular emphasis on 'informal' treatment, as embodied in the 1959 Mental Health Act, is seen partly in terms of an extension of social rights to mental patients, but also as necessary to create a universal and more effective mental health service. There is no essential conflict between a service which secures more efficient social rehabilitation, and one that meets the needs of users.

Needless to say this highly cheerful story of unmitigated progress has not gone unchallenged by those more critical of psychiatry and the state. One of the more pessimistic views is Andrew Scull's claim that the 'decarceration' of the mentally ill was promoted more by the needs of capitalism than the needs of users. A full employment economy had shrunk the underclass, and the availability of social security benefits made social integration a cheaper and more viable goal, while the emphasis on a more liberal approach derived from a need to develop more subtle forms of social control appropriate to a welfare rather than a Poor Law state. Scull argues that the aim was never to provide properly resourced community care but to discharge patients and save the expenditure being spent on the crumbling mental hospitals. The welfare state was generating more political demands for services than it could satisfy, resulting in a 'fiscal crisis of the state'. One solution to this was 'decarceration' or community care on the cheap, meaning the discharge of large numbers of ex-patients to the margins of society where they simply suffered a different form of social confinement, often actually ending up in prison (Scull, 1977).

Scull's account is helpful in drawing attention to wider economic influences on the shift to community care, but overstates its case. Gillian Dalley (1988) argues that there have been competing models of community care, each associated with particular sets of social interests. These are:

- *the client-focused model* which emphasises the need to maximise the rights of users to live an ordinary life in the community;
- *the professional practice model* favoured by the most powerful occupation-

al groups in the service, especially doctors, on the grounds of the more effective treatment that it is said will result;

- *the managerial planning model* with its pragmatic concern with planning priorities and cost savings that can be made by the rundown and closure of hospitals, often favoured by service managers and civil servants;
- *the informal care model* which may be emphasised by representatives of lay carers themselves, but becomes increasingly advocated by central government as a means of cheaper and supposedly more humane care.

Though one or other of the discourses associated with these models has been in the ascendant at particular times, none has been sufficiently dominant to exclude the others.

Joan Busfield (1986) offers a critical approach which also takes account of the interplay of the different interests around community care. She sees professional interests as initially predominant, with some if rather muted emphasis on users' interests. A two tier service emerged, she suggests, one in which professionals gave priority to acute patients in general hospital units, exacerbating the neglect and Cinderella status of long term patients in traditional mental hospitals. On the whole this professionally dominant model was accepted by the state, which emphasised the need for community services to back up hospital treatment. Contrary to Scull's argument, this meant that the growing state expenditure crisis of the 1970s *slowed down* the decarceration of mental patients, because the money for care in the community was not made available. It was only when state expenditure crises became particularly severe and there was also an ideological lurch to the right, that the managerial-planning and informal care models came to the fore. In a scenario not unlike that envisaged by Scull, the discharge of patients and rundown of institutions went ahead regardless (Carpenter and Williams, 1993). Professional preferences for 'acute' curative services had been reinforced by the 1962 Hospital Plan for England and Wales under which the Conservative government committed itself to a massive building programme of acute general hospitals, which was to be associated with a 'managerial-planning' run down of the NHS's care of the long term sick and disabled. Thus it was followed in 1963 by the White Paper *Health and Welfare: The Development of Community Care* which imposed a responsibility to provide community care on local authorities but provided no earmarked resources. As Richard Titmuss (1968) put it at the time community care was more of a 'fiction' than a 'fact'. The White Paper thus fitted into a professionally and increasingly managerially driven healthism, which has obvious parallels in the present day bracketing of reform of acute health and community care in the 1990 NHS and Community Care Act.

The shift to community care in mental health, though owing much to the extension of social rights after the Second World War, became defined primarily in terms of professional interests and priorities, in alliance with the 'new managerialism'; there was little emphasis on extending users' rights. During the 'consensus' era, governments accepted this model, but in reality did little to develop community based services. The 'new right' broke the stalemate in the 1980s.

## People with Learning Difficulties and Community Care

The 'client-focused' (what I call the 'user-centred') approach has arguably had much more influence upon the shift to community care for people with learning difficulties, because the link between institutionalisation and social control was particularly strong. This was highlighted in the early 1950s when the National Council for Civil Liberties lobbied strongly for the release of the many men and women whom they argued were wrongly incarcerated in mental deficiency colonies (Walmsley and Williams, 1990). The appropriateness of the biomedical model, and along with it the application of the sickness label to people with learning difficulties, and the supervision of doctors and nurses over their lives, was open to much greater challenge. By no stretch of the imagination were these institutions which 'treated' people, nor could they be made to do so by transforming them in line with liberal-professional principles.

Yet though the anti-institutional critique had particular relevance to their situation, in Britain at least it was not until the late 1960s that community care for people with learning difficulties became a live political issue. The 1959 Mental Health Act merely defined the grounds for compulsory detention of people with learning difficulties in greater detail, at a time when some other countries, particularly in Scandinavia, were enacting measures to extend their social rights (Tyne, 1982). Perhaps one reason was the fact that sociological and public interest in mental illness was very great. Mental health and illness are matters of potentially universal interest, and 1960s radicals like R D Laing in *The Politics of Experience* had even portrayed schizophrenia in glamorous terms as a form of social rebellion. Mental handicap however affected a 'social minority', lacked glamour, and consequently attracted much less sociological and public interest (Morris, 1969; Townsend, 1973; Bayley, 1973). What made the difference was the series of institutional scandals of the late 1960s and into the 1970s. These had ignited around conditions for older people in hospitals exposed by the publication of Barbara Robb's *Sans Everything* in 1968, but this also focused critical public attention on conditions in all long stay institutions. This included mental handicap hospitals, most notably the exposure and subsequent inquiry in 1969 into conditions at Ely and Farleigh Hospitals (Martin, 1984).

It is possible to question whether many positive benefits emerged from anti-institutional critiques and scandals (eg Jones, 1973; Sedgwick, 1982).

Yet while institutional scandals have been used as a convenient cover for those who on managerial planning grounds were simply looking for an excuse to close institutions down, and abandon their inmates to either sink or swim in the wider society, this effect should not necessarily be blamed on all institutional and professional critics. It is only properly applied to those, often of a new right persuasion who, like Thomas Szasz (1970), espouse a narrow civil liberties position concerned simply to remove institutional and professional oppression, without establishing social rights to any alternative means of support. This viewpoint cannot be attributed to most critics of institutional and professional power, who wished to improve and humanise services.

Thus the Ely Inquiry brought policy for people with learning difficulties into much more direct public focus, leading to the 1971 DHSS White Paper, *Better Services for the Mentally Handicapped,* which marked a distinct policy shift towards community care. Alan Tyne argues that though a considerable step forward, it was deficient in that it said nothing about the individual rights of users. The White Paper was also:

> weak in that it compromised its views on institutional care. To public and parental pressure it conceded that some half of the 60,000 or so people then in institutions should move into 'community care'. To medical, nursing and other pressures it conceded that substantial numbers (including 7,000 children) would always need the care 'which only a hospital can provide'. (Tyne, 1982, p.145).

In other words, bowing to powerful professional interests, the White Paper only partially articulated a user-centred model of care. It was not until the Jay Committee Report of 1979 that this professional model was officially challenged. As in the mental illness sector, replacement community services were slow to develop, though receiving some modest encouragement in the latter half of the 1970s by the development of jointly funded services between health and local authorities.

## Community Care for Older People

Many similar issues could be raised in relation to services for older people. While in theory the welfare state might seem a favourable context for an extension of the social rights of older people, progress was slow. Priority after the war, with the need to replace the lost population, was given to mothers and children, and from an economic point of view old people were not regarded as an investment for the future. As a result of such ageism, older people became disadvantaged clients of the welfare state, denied the same social rights as other people. In the NHS they received a Cinderella service whether from GPs or in general and mental hospitals (Henwood, 1990).

In the difficult post-war economic circumstances which confronted the 1945-51 Labour government, the Beveridge Report's proposal for subsistence level state pensions was one of the first items of the 'post-war settlement' to be jettisoned by the welfare state, and has never been implemented. The services which specifically addressed the needs of older people were, for reasons explained in the previous chapter, the public assistance institutions inherited from the Poor Law, many of them former workhouses which had simply changed their name. By the end of the 1950s these still accommodated three quarters of older people in residential care (Townsend, 1962).

So, even in a changed political environment favourable to a community approach, the persistence of ageism meant that the period up to the 1970s was largely one, as Roy Parker puts it, of 'stagnation' (Parker, 1990a). Hard pressed local authorities placed most emphasis on modernising the buildings, but not the social organisation of institutional care, and in any case made slow progress even towards this limited goal. There was however little public awareness or concern about the need to support frail older people in their homes, the assumption being that this was largely a family (and primarily a woman's) responsibility. In other words, there was at the time an implicit if not the later explicit emphasis on informal care. Thus it was not until the 1960s that local authorities were empowered to provide meals-on-wheels and home helps for older people. Domiciliary care for older people only gradually became available. Home helps originally helped women at home after maternity, under the 1918 Maternity and Child Welfare Act. During World War Two they became involved in giving care to a wider group of people, reinforced in discretionary powers given to local authorities under the 1946 National Health Service Act. However it was not until 1966 that they were given a statutory duty to provide home helps for older people (Land, 1991).

Parker argues that good intentions were much more in evidence in the latter half of the 1960s. With a reform-minded Labour government in power, the publication of *Sans Everything* indicating that not all was well with institutional provision, and sociological research like that by Peter Townsend and Dorothy Wedderburn (1965) indicating the existence of growing areas of unmet need, the omens looked more favourable. The new Social Services departments set up after the Seebohm Report in 1970 led to an increased expenditure and provision of domiciliary services for older people, though it has often been claimed that child care services received a greater priority. However, in the wake of the 1973 oil crisis, international recession, and the resulting public expenditure crisis of 1976, there were large central government cut backs in local authority expenditure. This in turn led to a curtailment of social services expenditure on older people, which was only partly eased by joint financing projects between local and health authorities. By the end of the 1970s, as Parker shows, local authority expenditure was still weighted as heavily if not more so towards residential care.

This is a very similar story for older people as for users of mental health services and people with learning difficulties, of a genuine but limited extension of social rights. For older people, this occurred particularly in the context of services which had always emphasised an informal care model of provision, backed up by institutional care only as a last resort for those who could demonstrate a pressing 'need' for it. The attempted extension of social rights to include domiciliary services and day care from the end of the 1960s only affected this situation at the margins. It also did very little to challenge the subordinate position of users and carers, whether in residential or community care. In most instances, the new social service departments were characterised by enhanced professional and managerial power, but very little increased community influence (Bolger, Corrigan, Docking and Frost, 1981).

Even so, this modest project to develop community care ran into serious difficulty during the expenditure crisis of the mid-1970s. We must also remember that this was occurring at a time of increasing need for social provision due to rapid demographic change, associated with a significant growth in the numbers of older people. The issue was not just, as Malcolm Wicks pointed out, that in 1901 one person in 20 was aged over 65 and that by 1981 it had increased to one in seven. It was also that, due to increasing longevity, people over 75 were more likely to need supporting services and care (Wicks, 1982).

The more explicit reassertion of an informal care model occurred in the confluence of these economic and demographic pressures. It is necessary to remember that the ideological shift rightwards began to occur after 1976 under the Labour government, before the Conservatives came to power in 1979 and articulated the approach more enthusiastically. For example, the 'Good Neighbour Campaign' of 1977, and the 1978 discussion document *A Happier Old Age*, were early anticipations of the more pronounced shift to care by the community in the 1980s. These were representative of the kinds of policy initiative which Phillip Abrams suspected were often an attempted 'colonisation' of the community. Central government was seeking to utilise the community as a complementary resource, and these policies were often implemented in hierarchical ways at local level by social service departments and voluntary agencies like the WRVS (Abrams, 1984). This too set a trend which was continued into the 1980s.

## A Waged Work and Union Perspective on these Developments

It cannot reasonably be claimed that public service unions, including COHSE, NALGO and NUPE did much to initiate the shift to community care in the 1950s. And when endorsing it in principle, trade unions and the labour movement did so in terms of the professional model developed by others rather than by formulating its own independent view or vision. This was certainly the case with COHSE, the union most directly affected by the shift to community care in mental health. As Shulamit Ramon points out, although COHSE President Claud Bartlett was a member of the Royal Commission that produced the 1957 Percy Report and subsequently the 1959 Mental Health Act, he did not play a particularly influential role and COHSE's evidence largely endorsed the professional practice or medical model of community care put forward by the psychiatrist members (Ramon, 1985, Ch 6). This was partly a product of the continuing alliance with psychiatrists which had been forged during the inter-war period. In addition, COHSE at this time was preoccupied with pay and conditions, at a time of falling recruitment to mental nursing which had been the result of post-war full employment. The union had become bogged down in a messy and only partially successful campaign of industrial action which, rather than seeking to link employment with wider service issues, focused largely on workers' immediate concerns (Carpenter, 1988, Ch 18).

Because of its preoccupation with mental hospital conditions, COHSE thus accepted, though was not particularly enthusiastic about, the new policy of community care. It doubted, correctly as it turned out, whether formal central government commitment to community care would be accompanied by sufficient resources to make the policy a reality. This was confirmed when the 1963 White Paper, *Health and Welfare: the Development of Community Care*, placed responsibilities on local authorities to provide community care for a more widely defined group of people than users of mental health services, but provided no earmarked central government funds. To some extent COHSE was quite reasonably concerned that this shift was a thinly disguised means by which central government intended to evade responsibility for community care. The union also claimed that it would lead to divided and uncertain administrative responsibilities between health and social services that would frustrate proper integrated planning.

Though these were reasonable concerns, COHSE and the nurses it represented were also influenced by a vested interest in hospital and NHS provision. At times this led sections of the membership to adopt defensive positions about conditions in hospitals, and attempts to expose the abuses and cruelties that arose from them. This involved efforts by older and established staff to cover up and even suppress justified attempts to 'whistle-blow' by younger and more idealistic student nurses (eg Martin, 1984; Beardshaw, 1982). It also sometimes led to rearguard actions against the development of community care, the last major occasion being when COHSE, along with the Royal College of Nursing and the nursing press, misguidedly campaigned against the proposals of the 1979 Jay Committee Report on the future of services for people with learning difficulties. This was because Jay, by rightly challenging the biomedical model, was seen to threaten the central position of nurses and the NHS in providing services for people with learning difficulties.

NUPE, however, was the one public service union in the early 1980s which took a positive approach to the proposed Jay reforms and demedicalisation of the care of people with learning difficulties. Doubtless this was influenced partly by its advocacy of a more social model of community care. However it was also the case that NUPE stood to gain as an organisation by the transfer of care into the local government community and residential care sector, where it had a more significant membership base than among mental handicap nurses. In other words, all organisations, trade unions and professional associations alike, responded to the reform of the care of people with learning difficulties in the light of their vested interests. They did not solely address themselves to the issue of what was in the best interests of users and their families.

Apart from the ethical indefensibility of this narrowly based trade union response (see also Sedgwick, 1982) it was shortsighted in that it meant that the trade union movement was often reacting to developments rather than playing an active role in shaping community care policies. It created the image of unions that were prepared to be militant when it came to pay and conditions, but were defensive over service issues.

In the local authority sector itself, the development of employment in community care was not only shaped by funding uncertainties, but also after 1970 by the emerging power relations in the new unified social services departments. We saw earlier how the psychiatric services themselves were increasingly rationalised under professional as well as managerial influence to give preference to the 'acutely ill' (Busfield, 1986). Similarly it could be argued that in the new social services departments, a division of labour was created in which management and professionals, whatever their disagreements with each other, effectively collaborated to downgrade community care, the user groups affected and those working in that sector in the power and status hierarchy. This heightened the existing divisions of class, gender, and 'race' associated with the occupational structures in the former health and welfare departments of local authorities.

Although it would take considerable space to delineate the complex cross-cutting lines of these divisions, the core of the whole structure was the professional hierarchy created around the new CQSW (Certificate of Qualification in Social Work) trained social workers. These not only dominated field social work, but also the 'periphery' of residential and domiciliary services where a mass of welfare assistants, care assistants, home helps, wardens and others worked with inferior terms and conditions of employment and career prospects. These were, and still are, reinforced by separate collective bargaining arrangements under the National Joint Industrial Council (NJIC) system which divides manual from professional and administrative staff in social services departments. While professional work is defined as intellectually demanding and responsible, and has pay and career prospects to match, manual work grades are perceived in much more downgraded terms as involved in routine and less skilled work, with associated poor pay and short job ladders. These social divisions were reinforced by 'grade' trade unionism, with manual workers joining the National Union of Public Employees (NUPE) and the Transport and General Workers' Union (TGWU), and administrative and professional workers mainly joining the National and Local Government Officers' Association (NALGO).

This division led to the undervaluing of direct caring work within social services departments, in both homes and domiciliary services; work which was particularly likely to performed by women and black people. This was reinforced by lack of power and access to professional training. Professional qualifications, particularly the Certificate of Qualification in Social Work (CQSW) – now replaced by the Diploma in Social Work (DSW) – were not just means of staking out job autonomy, but also a prerequisite for progress up the rapidly extending hierarchies in social service departments.

Thus within social work there was particular emphasis by professionals and managers on child protection work, reflected in resources and numbers of qualified staff, in comparison with field work with users of mental health services, people with learning difficulties, and older people. This was particularly pronounced in the case of older people. For though work with users of mental health services had some professional kudos, and work with people with learning difficulties was seen as involving education and training, work with older people, especially in residential care, was likely, as the Wagner Report (1988) put it, to be seen in peripheral terms – merely as 'tending'. This was also reflected in the pronounced social class, gender and 'race' divisions to be found, particularly in the residential sector. Whereas in other sectors CQSW-trained staff were likely to be engaged in an active 'therapeutic' role, their position in homes for older people was much more likely to be defined as managerial (Parry, Rustin, and Satyamurti, 1979; Howe, 1986; Hallet, 1989; Carpenter, Elkan, Leonard, and Munro, 1991).

## 'Border disputes' and Community Care

The final issue to consider, at least in passing, is how 'border disputes' between agencies, professions and occupations have shaped patterns of community care for good or ill. These are often of a highly complex nature, not only because of the shifting alliances and disputes which occur between professions and occupations, but also because they are also often riven by internal factional strife (Bucher and Strauss, 1966). With this in view, what is offered below is inevitably an oversimplified account of professions in community care.

In the period under review, from the 1950s to the end of the 1970s, a professional practice model of community care was, I have argued, largely pre-eminent. This had the intended effect of placing control over the development and implementation of community care mainly in the hands of 'professional experts', rather than local or national politicians, or users of services. The main external political control exercised from above was, as we have seen, over funding, for which central government took hardly any responsibility.

An important consequence of this shift was the increasing friction between the agencies and professions involved, which initially intensified as local authority social service departments became increasingly important community care providers. This became more problematic as collaborative joint funding ventures between health and local authorities became more common in the late 1970s. Whether as cause or consequence, this involved a change in the professional discourse underlying the provision of community care, eroding the influence of the more mechanistic 'medical' model in favour of the more holistic 'social' model. This in turn led to a shift in power from the professions grouped in alliance around one model, to those grouped around the other, from psychiatry to professional social work respectively.

The extent to which such a shift has taken place should not be exaggerated. While the Mental Health Act of 1983 enhanced the role of 'approved social workers', it did not fundamentally encroach on the professional dominance of psychiatrists. There is some evidence that community psychiatric nurses have experienced considerable uncertainties and confusions, and conflicting loyalties. In 1982 the changed syllabus for Registered Mental Nurse (RMN) training substantially shifted the emphasis from a medical to a social model. What empirical evidence is available suggests however that adherence to the medical model of mental illness remained strong, and exerted an influence over community psychiatric nurses' approach to their work (Woolf, Goldberg and Fryers, 1988; Woolf and Goldberg, 1988; Sheppard, 1990).

Throughout this period, professional 'team work' and interagency collaboration became the favoured solutions in the increasing areas of overlapping health and welfare work. However, as Gillian Dalley (1989) points out this has proved difficult to work successfully, not just because of the 'structural' complexity of the organisations involved, but because of the barriers erected by competing professional ideologies. Dalley's survey during the mid-1980s of 236 health and social services workers showed that conflicts between general practitioners and social workers were the most common, but inter-occupational hostilities manifested themselves in all possible permutations. Social workers often attributed their conflicts with nurses to the latter's perceived subservience to doctors.

The expectation that a more social approach to community care would simply happen by getting the relevant professions together across the health and social service divide was therefore naive, not just because of the organisational complexities involved, but also because differences in professional orientation and outlook were scarcely considered. In addition, whether in health or social services, the professions concerned gave a low priority to those with long term needs for care. Both health and social service professions had a pronounced 'acute' bias, linked to their wider social role in the welfare state in prioritising 'socially productive' forms of intervention which do not represent a fundamental challenge to the status quo. So while medicine has been biased towards cure, to the neglect of both prevention and care, social service professions have been similarly biased towards individual 'therapeutic' interventions. Not only have these often failed to address the social causes of social problems, as radical social work critics have long argued, they have also served to marginalise the needs of those with longer term needs for care or support in the community, including many older people, people with learning difficulties and users of mental health services.

## What About the Users?

One must however be cautious before accepting that one model, and hence one set of professionals, is 'superior' to another, for two reasons. First, the social model was used as a vehicle for professional social work to enhance its power, prestige, and financial rewards in relation to other more disadvantaged social services staff, as well as other traditionally subordinated professions such as nursing. Second, though the adoption of a social model of community care might generally be seen as more appropriate to people's holistic needs, and help to facilitate a more participative partnership with users, this does not happen automatically. As has often been pointed out (eg Jones, 1983; Clarke, 1988), social workers are often embroiled in controlling relations with users, for example as underlined by their legislative powers to 'section' people under the 1983 Mental Health Act and to remove children from their parents. Even where these formal powers do not exist, social workers' professional ideology may lead them to act as if they know what is in users' best interests, and offer few choices, as Alan Tyne found in his study of social services for people with learning difficulties (Tyne, 1978). It is very likely that this was part of the general pattern of social services provision in community care (for example, see Beresford and Croft, 1981).

Professional world views are only one influence on work behaviour. Gillian Dalley (1989) found, in the survey referred to earlier, that despite significant contrasts in professional ideologies, there was greater commonality in the way that public service workers made sense of their daily work dilemmas. For example, at an ideological level, doctors in her survey tended to view care as a family responsibility, while social workers more often put emphasis on users' rights to services through the state. However in practice both groups, and public services workers generally, were likely as a result of their position in the 'front line' at the 'sharp end' of practice, to come independently to shared views which differed from service managers at a higher level more removed from direct practice. Sometimes this led them into a less restrained advocacy of users' interests, though it could also lead them to experience pressure from users which might be explained in terms of 'unreasonable' demands, and that clients had contributed to their own problems. Therefore in both positive and negative senses, daily work perceptions may be more similar than different between health and social services personnel, than might seem the case from publicly espoused professional viewpoints.

In short, by the end of the 1970s, the professional and pressure group alliances grouped around social and more medical ideologies of community care may have battled it out on behalf of users and their families, but there is not much evidence of attempts by any participants to seek the active involvement of users in decision-making and teamwork. As we shall see, it was the failures of this fragmented pattern of professionally dominated care which helped to precipitate community care reform in the 1980s, culminating in the 1990 community care reforms. In retrospect, the 1970s may be seen as the heyday of professional power, though under increasing challenge from both left and right. As the new right now attacks professional power in the name of consumerism, one of the most crucial issues for the labour movement and the left is the extent to which new alliances can be forged between rival professionals, other public service workers and users, aimed at achieving a genuine sharing of power among workers in ways that also foster accountability to users (see Wilding, 1981).

Professionals have often been rightly criticised for seeking to stake out and defend an area of privileged autonomy, by mystifying not only their expertise but also their extent of adherence to occupationally-patrolled principles of ethical conduct. Nevertheless, as Michael Hill (1982) points out, the notion of altruistic public service cannot be entirely dismissed out of hand. Indeed it is something which has already put the medical profession at odds with a Conservative government which is seeking, through the creation of the NHS internal market, to erode the underlying altruistic principles of the service. But that does not mean simply supporting professions when they are under attack unless they, in turn, are prepared to agree to the establishment of a genuine partnership with other workers and accountability to users.

The next chapters of this book look more closely at such issues in the context of the community care reforms initiated since the Conservatives came to power in 1979, and the alternatives to them.

# Chapter 3
# The road to community care reform

I have argued that the shift to community care was a response to the changed political and economic circumstances associated with the coming of the welfare state after the Second World War. The emphasis on community care as a social right was, however, qualified by the limited commitment to social rights in general. Social rights to community care were also further qualified by the way in which welfare state professionals succeeded in imposing therapeutic and integrationist definitions of 'need'. Even so this 'professional-practice' model was only partly implemented in the 1960s and early 1970s. By the late 1970s, as we have seen, it was becoming increasingly challenged by a managerial planning model, allied to an explicit rather than the previous implicit preference for informal care.

## The 'Doomsday Scenario' in Community Care?

It is plausible to argue that these developments, culminating in the 1990 reforms, are largely a new right inspired attack on public provision in community care, falsely represented as a new deal for users, for two main reasons. First, by romanticising family care as an ideal over institutional provision, the new politics of community care reinforces the traditional image of the nuclear family, where caring is assumed to be dutifully and sensitively performed by wives or other female relatives (Graham, 1983). Such a view undoubtedly helps to sanction the more rapid rundown of institutions, and discharge of their residents, on the grounds not only that it will save money but also that people will be better cared for in the bosom of the family, and be better able to lead a 'normal' life. At a time of high unemployment, this is deemed to be appropriate work for women, especially in the context of a new right (and now Labour 'right') discourse which partly blames national decay on the supposed erosion of the traditional family.

Linked to this is the growing 'pragmatic' preoccupation with older people as the prime concern of policy for community care, the continuing growth in numbers of whom it is presumed will generate demands that the state could not possibly meet on its own. As part of this, there is not just a retreat from the state back to the family, but a retreat from the state to the voluntary and commercial sectors. The 1989 White Paper, *Caring for People*, which preceded the 1990 Act, defined community care in its opening paragraph as:

> the services and support which people... need to be able to live as independently as possible in their own homes, or in 'homely' settings in the community.

It thus defines community care as also involving 'homely' institutional care, and there is no doubt that the voluntary and commercial sectors are seen as better able to provide this than the local state. This ideological assault by the new right is, as we shall see, matched by a funding system which is profoundly biased in favour of the commercial sector and against the local state, and which seeks increasingly to confine its role to purchasing and regulating, rather than directly providing care, a process Alan Walker (1993) describes as the 'residualisation' of the public sector. In this sense the 1990 community care reforms are much more an engine of privatisation than the NHS reforms, even though the latter have attracted much more public concern on these grounds.

If a new right agenda is the main thrust behind community care since the 1980s, it is equally plausible to represent it as a 'doomsday scenario' for community care in which a managerial planning model of 'community care on the cheap' predominates. With some justification, it is thus possible to argue that the 'decarceration' process envisaged by Andrew Scull is finally being realised. Large numbers of people are being made to walk the plank of hospital and institutional discharge into communities that have been reeling from the effects of deindustrialisation and the growth of poverty, and the 'capping' of local authority expenditure, adding to the strain on real families as opposed to the mythical 'family'. Such pressures have particularly but not solely borne upon women as main family carers, as intensified by class and 'race' (Graham, 1993), the collapse of full employment, and the widening of social inequalities characteristic of the emergence of the 'two thirds, one third' society since the 1980s (Therborn, 1989).

As a result of these changes, significant numbers of people have ended up either as ex-mental patients on skid row or even in prison, or (especially for older people who couldn't afford better) preyed upon by entrepreneurs who saw the chance of a making a quick buck out of the burgeoning residential care industry. At the end of this cycle, users were either no better or worse off, condemned to live excluded lives on the margins of society and to suffer abuse from police, or within overburdened families, or in private homes whose regimes were only nominally accountable to public scrutiny.

This is certainly part of the picture as research from a variety of sources, including public service unions, has shown. For example, the uncertain fate of former mental hospital residents, and the poor quality of much commercial residential care, has been highlighted by research by Robert Quick as a COHSE Regional Secretary in the East Midlands undertaken in the late 1980s (personal communication). Research jointly commissioned by NUPE West Midlands Division and the West Midlands County Council (1986), the first of its kind undertaken, sought to systematically uncover patterns of practice in the commercial residential sector in the West Midlands. It found that whilst some homes are run to high standards

> ... many fall well below any acceptable standards of decency and are a disgrace. In such homes, almost untouched by legislation, ill treatment, indignity and abuse are a daily occurrence – and a highly profitable one for the owners (p. 1).

This concern was reinforced by research conducted with NALGO by Harriet Harman MP and Sarah Harman (1989) into the first ninety six cases investigated under the Registered Homes Act 1984. The Act itself had been a belated response to the public concern expressed over the unregulated but state funded expansion of commercial care. The Report highlighted both the often scandalous conditions in homes, and the woefully inadequate official inspection machinery:

> There is evidence of abuse, binding residents with cord, misuse of drugs, fraud, fire hazard, lack of hygiene, and a sorry tale of bruised and miserable residents.

The Report also questioned whether much commercial residential care was appropriate. It quoted a survey of 351 patients carried out by the British Geriatrics Society in private nursing homes in the Avon area which revealed that many elderly persons were being admitted to residential care with problems that could be reversed and coped with in their own homes.

These concerns had also been expressed in *Time for Justice*, a NUPE (1986) Report on the care of older people. This not only drew attention to the inadequacies in the enforcement of standards under the 1984 legislation, but also to the fact that these regulations are concerned primarily with technical requirements (fire precautions, building codes, control of dangerous drugs) and staffing levels rather than with standards of care. Nursing homes may operate quite legitimately without any reference to principles of dignity, autonomy, quality of the resident's life or individual choice.

It is not however the total picture, for two reasons. First, the doomsday scenario can easily obscure the previous shortcomings of state services and earlier failures to develop community care. The previous chapter examined some of the reasons for these:

- central government in the period after the 1962 Hospital Plan largely placed duties on local authorities to provide community care, without clearly defining what it meant;
- on the rare occasions when it did, as in the Chronically Sick and Disabled Persons Act 1970, it provided no proper machinery for ensuring that local authorities fulfilled their statutory obligations;
- the slow and uneven response by local authorities themselves, who had 'more important' priorities and in any case became increasingly cash-strapped from the mid-1970s;
- the low priority given to community care within social services departments;
- the inadequacies of local authority residential provision;
- the attempt by staff in the long stay hospitals to defend their institutions and/or their occupations.

There was thus a need for radical change to break the stalemate over community care that had developed due to political inertia and professional lack of interest or opposition.

Second, the doomsday scenario can be misleading because it fails to acknowledge that the new right and welfare profiteers have not entirely had their own way. Public service unions like COHSE, NALGO and NUPE and other campaigners in the 1980s have managed to prevent the worst effects of decarceration policies, compared with what has happened in the United States. Though it was insufficient to meet growing needs, health and social service expenditure has been relatively protected (Baldock, 1989; Evandrou, Falkingham and Glennerster, 1990). Massive retrenchment in other areas of public expenditure has had profound implications for health and social care, most notably in housing (Hills and Mullings, 1990). There have been undoubted benefits from community care policies, including enhanced quality of life in the community for former residents of long stay hospitals (Tomlinson, 1991, Ch 6) and enhanced access to residential care for older people through social security support. By the end of the 1980s it was clear that the welfare state's role had been restructured and redefined, but it had not been abolished or privatised to the extent demanded by the far right, for example, along the lines of the government's think tank proposals of 1983 leaked by the *Economist* magazine.

### 'Welfare Pluralism' – the New Consensus?

This restructuring has come increasingly to be seen as 'welfare pluralism' (Johnson, 1988), which was consolidated, at least for the time being, under John Major's premiership – though the renewed crisis caused by economic slump in the 1990s, and the associated public expenditure deficit, is leading to a renewed and more explicitly right wing onslaught on state welfare. It is important to realise that welfare pluralism has both positive and negative aspects. The negative side is the partial retreat from public provision by the encouragement of a plurality of providers, through an expansion of lay 'caring networks', and commercial and voluntary provision in place of the state. At the same time the state itself has been progressively restructured in order to make it obey market disciplines, partly to contain costs, but also from an ideological hostility to the public sector, and the people who work for it through what Hunter (1993) calls 'new public management'.

Yet though it represented a shift to the right which used the twin pressures of demographic change and economic difficulties as justification, there was, in principle at least, a more progressive aspect to welfare pluralism which sought to create more decentralised, individualised, and user-sensitive services (Hadley and Hatch, 1981). Thus welfare pluralism has also put the issue of the quality and responsiveness of services at the centre of the debates about public provision. As critics, including public service unions, often rightly pointed out, there has, in practice, been more of a managerialist emphasis on privatisation, cost containment and getting more for the same amount of money than ensuring quality and responsiveness. Where measures of quality are put forward, they are often crude, and take little account of the complexity of 'performance criteria' in the human services or of environmental influences such as class, 'race' and gender on provision. Users are rarely, if ever, consulted about quality measures. Nevertheless, much more attention has been focused on questioning what the public services should do, in ways that potentially open up a radical agenda for reform of the worst effects of bureaucracy and professional dominance associated with the welfare state from the 1940s to the end of the 1970s, as long as it is not seen as a substitute for providing adequate resources.

It is therefore the case, as Alan Walker (1993) has claimed, that the benefits of 'welfare pluralism' have been exaggerated by its proponents. Walker questions the enthusiasm of Day and Klein (1987), among others, who have welcomed the shift of local authorities from a providing to a regulating role, and by implication the enhanced choice, efficiency and responsiveness that is presumed to come from breaking the state monopoly in provision and opening it up to competition. As he suggests, restrictions since 1985 on social security support, and the failure to sufficiently up-rate it in line with inflation, squeezed standards in private residential care and led in many instances to supplementary charges which users and their families could ill-afford. Also, as we saw above, the research conducted by public service unions in the 1980s called into question the quality of much of that commercial provision, and whether it was appropriate. Yet whatever the arguments made in favour of welfare pluralism, the government's community care reforms, as we shall see in the next chapter, do not involve a genuine pluralism in which the public can engage in even-handed competition with commercial and voluntary provision. Instead the rules of the 'mixed economy of care' have been stacked heavily against the public sector.

One of the reasons why the government has been able to get away with this sleight of hand is because they have to some extent been able to construct a consensus for their general approach beyond the ranks of the new right, to include those whom George and Wilding (1985) call 'reluctant collectivists'. These are a varied group of non socialist reformists who have traditionally held that the efficient workings of the market must be complemented by necessary state intervention, but who in the 1980s have partially accepted the new right's critique of the welfare state and call for more decentralised services with a greater role for private provision (for example, Hadley and Hatch, 1981; Bosanquet, 1983). However they have also been able to construct this consensus because this critique has a genuine validity in the light of the past failings of bureaucratically and professionally dominated health and welfare services, which were highlighted in relation to community care in the previous chapter. The challenge for the left is not to defend existing community care, but to show how decentralised models of public provision, which genuinely empower users, can work without resorting significantly to market provision and the commodification of public care.

One consequence of the new right's need to construct a consensus with the 'welfare pluralists' is that they have had to concede ground. In the case of both the NHS and community care reforms they have had to at least pretend that they have been seeking both to improve the quality and responsiveness of public services, and maintain access to services as a social right. Indeed, as far as community care is concerned, we need to acknowledge that the government has extended rights to services in principle – though as we shall see to a considerably lesser degree in reality – in services which previously were characterised by professional and bureaucratic dictation of needs. In doing so, Tory governments have raised the issue of citizen participation in health and welfare in a more direct and potentially enforceable way.

The way that the government sees this operating is by means of an alliance between the central government, managers, and 'consumers'. While the managerial reforms of the NHS and social services in the 1970s were inspired by an industrial model which took no account of the human services context in health and welfare, the government in the 1980s was, in drawing on the expertise of people like Griffiths and Rayner, more cleverly seeking to apply the supposedly more 'people-sensitive' methods of the retail sector of capitalism. The success of government policies can also be tested against this second meaning of 'pluralism', that it leads to more pluralistic structures, which deliver services of high quality, which are decentralised, individualised, and offer choices to users.

In short, though the government was in part seeking to pursue a new right agenda, the possibility of a US-style doomsday scenario for community care has to some extent galvanised opposition and led to reforms which have some progressive aspects. That is not to deny the negative and disguised effects of massive under-resourcing and privatisation in undermining these progressive possibilities, but it is to acknowledge that aspects of the community care reforms should be defended, such as the shift from medical to social care and from the unaccountable NHS to local government, and above all to a needs-based system emphasising user entitlements, participation and choice.

The Griffiths Report of 1988, *Community Care: Agenda for Action*, emerged out of a growing awareness of the inadequacies of community care policies in the 1980s, in terms of appropriate provision, sensitivity to users' needs and lack of co-ordination between the agencies concerned. There were two main sets of issues, the growing crisis in community provision for residents of long stay mental illness and mental handicap hospitals, and the increasingly inadequate and chaotic provision of domiciliary and residential care for older people. To some extent of course these are overlapping and not separate issues, as older people are significant users of mental health services.

## Mental Health Services and Community Care Reform

In his famous 'water tower' speech of 1961, Enoch Powell as Minister of Health had predicted that as a result of the drugs 'revolution' and the liberalisation associated with the 1959 Mental Health Act, the closure of the traditional mental hospitals would be completed within 15 years. Events were to prove him wrong. While there was a significant rundown in beds, and some transfer to more intensively used District General Hospital units, the traditional mental hospital proved a remarkably resilient institution. The Labour government's 1976 White Paper, *Priorities for Health and Personal Social Services in England* in the midst of

the severe expenditure crisis externally imposed by the International Monetary Fund, had insisted that there was no particular policy to close long stay mental illness and mental handicap hospitals. It realised that in the context of local government cutbacks, it was not legitimate to expect that replacement services could be developed in the community. The Conservative government after 1979, in worse economic circumstances, pressed ahead with a closure programme regardless through its 1981 Care in the Community initiative (DHSS, 1981, 1983; Busfield, 1986).

The relationship of these policies to the biomedical model of care varied. For people with learning difficulties the 1979 Jay Report's valid questioning of the medical model, and optimistic view that many residents of hospitals could lead independent lives in the community, served as a justification for seeking closure of such institutions. For users of mental health services the increasing dominance of the biomedical model of mental illness unwittingly played into the hands of 'managerial planning' advocates of closure. There was a consistency running through Conservative approaches from Enoch Powell, through Keith Joseph, to the 1981 initiative. Keith Joseph had argued in 1971 that:

> Psychiatry is to join the rest of medicine… the treatment of psychosis, neurosis, and schizophrenia have been entirely changed by the drugs revolution. People go into hospital with mental disorders and they are cured (quoted by Jones, 1988, p.35)

The idea was that long stay hospitals would close and people be admitted to District General Hospital units for short periods, before returning to normal life as normal people. As Peter Barham (1992) points out, this model simply regarded the community as a 'null' place. As Kathleen Jones (1988, p.83) points out, it ignored the role of human emotions and social influences on mental health. It is thus a model which requires the minimum response from the wider society.

The government pressed ahead and there was a rapid fall in beds, though it was not until 1985 that the first hospital closed – Banstead in Surrey. In the 10 years from 1976 to 1986 the numbers of residents in mental illness hospitals fell from 109,000 to 82,500, and in mental handicap hospitals from 59,000 to 42,000, much of this occurring after 1979 (Walker, 1989, p.211). By 1989, mental illness beds had fallen to 56,200 (Cooke and Ford, 1992). It would be unfair to suggest that no replacement facilities were provided. Central government both exerted heavy pressure on health authorities to produce timetables for closure, and at the same time facilitated a greater transfer of resources from health to social services. Nevertheless concern grew that the rapid implementation of decarceration policies was leading to a doomsday scenario in community care, brought sharply into focus by the publication of the report of the House of Commons Select Committee on Social Services (1985). This drew attention to the negative effects of decarceration, and in terms reminiscent of Andrew Scull it argued that:

> Large numbers are sleeping rough in archways and under railway bridges, some within hailing distance of the Palace of Westminster (paragraph 142).

Many, it was claimed, ended up in prison because there was no suitable alternative. These effects were the result of a policy which put the cart before the horse by pushing ahead with closure without ensuring that adequate reprovision was available. Above all the report challenged the notion that community care can be 'cost-neutral', and reasserted the need for properly resourced and staffed care in the community. The Select Committee's Report led to a shift of emphasis towards requiring health authorities to ensure that reprovision was available before mental hospital residents were discharged into the community, which has subsequently led in the 1990s to 'discharge planning' and the 'care programming' approach (Thornicroft et al, 1993).

These themes were taken up by the Audit Commission the following year in its 1986 report, *Making a Reality of Community Care.* This was mainly concerned, as we shall see, with the growth of residential care for older people. However it also criticised the government's approach to the rundown of the mental illness and mental handicap hospitals. The report emphasised the effects of government financial 'capping' of local authorities and the inadequate mechanisms for transferring resources across from health authorities, as major problems preventing the development of community reprovision. Where successful services had been established across the health and social services divide this was often attributed to the dynamic leadership of a few individuals determined to break the local deadlock. The system based on community mental health centres in Torbay, Devon, was one of those singled out for praise – though the report made no mention of the positive role that the local COHSE branch and south-west regional office of the union had played in bringing it to fruition.

The Audit Commission report was a prime influence on the review that led to the report by Sir Roy Griffiths in 1988, *Community Care: an Agenda for Action.* Griffiths was similarly preoccupied with the development of state-funded commercial care for older people. However he did insist that mental hospital closures should proceed carefully, and no individual discharged without clear arrangements being made for their continuing care. From this a model of the continuing involvement of the NHS, with ring-fenced funds made available, emerged as part of the 1990 reforms, which were distinctly different from the arrangements for community care as a whole. However, there was a catch in that local authorities needed to put up 30 per cent of the money in order to qualify for the 'specific grant', and only a limited and inadequate pot of money is being made available (Butler, 1993).

This preferential treatment can be put down to a number of influences, including the power of the psychiatrists' lobby, and genuine concern for the welfare of discharged residents, and awareness of the particular pressures that community care in mental health places on carers (see Perring, 1989). It is also however a consequence of the perceived need for social control of those diagnosed as mentally ill, and the continuing lack of social acceptability of people with 'strange' behaviour. There is by no means as great a concern about ensuring services are provided for people with learning difficulties, perhaps partly because they are now regarded as much more of a 'burden' than, as in the inter-war period, a 'threat'.

For whatever reasons, government policy at best merits two cheers in that the worst excesses of decarceration have been avoided in Britain, even if there is a continuing and pronounced 'care gap'. Dylan Tomlinson (1991) argues that on the whole the closure of mental hospitals in the 1980s has largely been well planned and regulated, with resourcing of a significant if still not sufficient amount of community 'reprovision' at least for the ageing group of former residents of long stay institutions. Community provision is less well developed for users in younger age groups who are more often treated for short interludes in District General Hospital units before discharge to an uncertain fate into the community, the effects of which are wrongly blamed on closure programmes (Tomlinson, 1992). Other studies have confirmed the existence of a considerable care gap (Chapman, Goodwin and Hennelly, 1991), including COHSE's report on the situation in London at the end of the 1980s (Lister, 1991). There is thus no room for complacency. Because no proper follow up statistics are kept, as Lew Chester points out, very little is known about the fate of those discharged, and estimates that one in three of men and half the women in Britain's prisons have psychiatric problems gives cause for alarm (Chester, 1992). One of the few follow-up studies showed that ex-patients' contact with judicial authorities often occurred because their behaviour was disturbing to people around them. Courts are sentencing former patients to custody against central government advice since 1990, and there is growing evidence that this is more likely to happen to black users of mental health services. The problems lie partly in lack of liaison between agencies, and the inadequacy of benefits, housing provision, and other services (Cooke and Ford, 1992; Sone, 1990).

Such developments, rather than leading as they should to improved community provision, are slowing down the shift to community care. Negative campaigns against hospital closure like those mounted by SANE (*Schizophrenia: A National Emergency*), have not helped. Tapping widespread NIMBY (Not In My Back Yard) sentiments, they have mobilised around neg-

ative labels of mental health service users as mad and potentially dangerous people. They have been vigorously opposed by a progressive alliance
involving trade unions, MIND and other organisations, but there is evidence
that they have had a strong influence on government policy (Bartlett,
1989a, 1989b). In the 1980s there was a growing polarisation among pressure and interest groups in mental health, according to the extent to
which they gave priority to user self-determination, or emphasised the
need for professional or legal protection. Groups representing the views
of psychiatrists and apprehensive relatives were more likely to be found in
the latter camp (Pilgrim, 1993). Anne Rogers and David Pilgrim (1991)
argue that user groups in the British Mental Health Users Movement
(MHUM) have had a considerable degree of success in challenging the biomedical model and advancing the cause of self-advocacy.

As well as this, economic and social realities are likely to slow the closure
programme. Closure and reprovision was often financed from specula-
tive land sales associated with the 1980s property boom. Furthermore, the
financial state of local authorities is now even more parlous in an era of economic depression and government capping, a point of some importance
to which I will return.

Reprovision in the community has therefore at best been a qualified success, at least for former residents of long stay institutions. There is less evidence, however, in mental health services of a general shift to more positive policies of 'empowerment' associated at least with the rhetoric of the
community care reforms as a whole. Thus Dylan Tomlinson is more critical of the failure of managers and professionals to actively involve, rather
than merely consult, users about replacement services. Other critics have
argued that the shift to community mental health centres can often involve
a relocation of psychiatrists' powers, without genuine involvement and
accountability to users (Tudor, 1990/91). The mental health services remain hierarchical and highly medicalised, and have been only partially reformed by the 1983 Mental Health Act. By making an exception of it, Griffiths and the community care reforms as a whole have helped to reinforce
these tendencies. The struggle is therefore not just for more resources to
close the care gap, but also for a shift to a democratised and less medicalised mental health service which would combat labelling, maximise
'self-advocacy' by users, and tackle the wider causes of mental distress associated with social inequalities of gender, class and 'race'; for example,
as envisaged by Peter Barham, (1992, Ch 5), the Socialist Health Association
1989), and user groups like Survivors Speak Out (Rogers, Pilgrim and
Lacey, 1992).

The continuing dominance of the biomedical model in mental health
community care is reflected in the continuing influence of psychiatrists
upon government, which in the near future may be reflected in legislation
to impose some form of compulsory community supervision on users of

mental health services, against the opposition of most other significant pressure groups and the House of Commons Health Services Select Committee. By contrast there has been a pronounced shift away from biomedical approaches and services for people with learning difficulties and which, though leaving much more to be done, has led to very real improvements in services since the early 1980s (Booth, 1990).

## Older People and Community Care Reform

There is no doubt that increasing official concern at the implications of an 'ageing' society and the failure of a co-ordinated government response to social provision was the chief stimulus to community care reform in the 1980s. Although the majority of people over 65 years report their health as good, older people – particularly those aged over 85 years – are more likely to use services more intensively, and have a greater need for care as a result of some mental or physical disability (Sinclair and Williams, 1990; Victor, 1991). Resources that older people can draw on themselves are affected by family structure, residence and their financial position. Most people get poorer as they get older, but the extent to which this happens is a consequence of the gender, 'race' and class inequalities which continue to afflict people later in their lives, affecting both their extent of need and ability to meet it out of their own resources. As the research review by Parker, Sinclair and Williams (1990, p.65) concluded:

> In general therefore old people do not have much money to spend on services. Those among them who have most need of services are particularly likely to be badly off.

The numbers of older people from 1901 to 1981 as a percentage of the total population has significantly increased:

|      | 65+  | 85+  |
|------|------|------|
| 1901 | 4.7  | 0.15 |
| 1951 | 10.9 | 0.45 |
| 1981 | 15.0 | 1.03 |

Official projections suggest that by 2025 nearly 19 per cent of the population will be over 65 years, and 2.28 per cent over 85 years (Leathard, 1990, p.112). It is this convergence between the growth in numbers of older people, their greater need for services, their relative lack of personal resources and the wider crisis in the welfare state, that set the alarm bells ringing in government policy-making circles, and led to the 1990 reforms.

The authors of these reforms claim that it is both to be a managerial rationalisation of existing provision to make sure it is used in more appropriate and cost effective ways, and a means of extending social rights and choice to community care for users denied them by the previous system

Yet it only achieves the latter to a limited degree. As far as older people are concerned, the reforms are much more concerned with rationing. This was largely inevitable given a very narrowly based review which was preoccupied with managerial issues within existing resources, and failed to situate community care in a wider framework of social policy for older people. Thus such crucially important issues as the increasing economic constraints on local government, the existing inadequacy of pensions provisions for older

people, and the likely future effects of the phasing out of State Earnings Related Pensions (SERPS), were not made part of the Griffiths brief.

The first aim of policy has been to rein in institutional health care provision for older people under the NHS. Large numbers of older people have occupied health service beds because of the lack of suitable residential alternatives, or because their health care needs had not been dealt with earlier. The aim has been to ensure health care needs are more often met in the community by primary care services, and that needs for residential care ('social' rather than 'medical' care) are provided outside the NHS, if necessary by local authorities, but preferably by commercial and voluntary organisations.

There is nothing in itself objectionable about de-medicalising the care of older people, where it can be shown to be appropriate. NHS wards are not often homely places, and few quick-fix cures can be offered by health professionals. The influence of the biomedical model means that it is more likely that physical needs will be given a greater priority than emotional and social needs. Similarly, more attention to primary care might ensure that fewer older people end up in hospital. The danger however is that such policies may be cost rather than need-driven, and encourage the view that older people and/or their relatives are 'misusing' the NHS. This could be seen as a further erosion of principles of universal access to the NHS, by questioning the right of older people to use health services to a much greater extent than occurs with younger people. As Mark Thomas (1993) has pointed out, a major reason why the government wishes to shift responsibility from medical to social care is because the former is more often considered a social right than the latter.

We should not in this context ignore the effects of the NHS reforms, which were not accidentally hitched together in 1990 with community care. Many commentators have suggested that the effect of the NHS internal market will be to encourage the intensive use of acute beds, to the neglect of provision of people with longer term health needs in 'Cinderella' specialties like psychiatry and geriatrics (for example, Lunn, 1989). While the government sought the rapid implementation of the internal market in the NHS, implementation of the financial provisions of the community care reforms was delayed until April 1993. In other words, the rundown of care in the NHS was given a much higher priority than ensuring replacement services were available in the community. It is also becoming apparent that despite this delay in implementation, many local authorities will not be ready to operate what will be complex assessment and contracting proceedings under the Act, involving a major shift in the organisation and culture of social services departments (Brindle, 1992; Clode, 1992; Hudson, 1992). On top of this, they will also be pretty hard up for cash!

To this extent then, rather than representing a new era of social rights in community care, the 1990 reforms might lead to its greater marginalisation first within the NHS, and second by shifting care from the responsibility of central government, and over to local government, commercial and voluntary sectors; as Gerald Wistow (1988) puts it 'off-loading responsibilities for care'. Such a shift, dressed up in the language of need and sensitivity to individual rights, could in some senses be seen as reinforcing an ageist and healthist approach to social policy which gives first priority to acute health care needs.

The second central feature of the reforms is their attempt to ensure the administrative and financial rationalisation of community care 'within the resources available' by placing the lead co-ordinating responsibility on local authorities (paragraph 1.3). Sir Roy Griffiths in his 1988 report accepted the Audit Commission's view that the previous system, particularly the unregulated expansion of residential care in the 1980s, had created a system of 'perverse incentives' encouraging residential care. As we saw in the previous chapter, a bias in favour of residential care had always existed, because of the lack of priority given to provision of domiciliary services. The most characteristic feature of the 1980s was not only a huge expansion in residential care, but also an accompanying shift away from the state and voluntary to the commercial sectors, as the table below illustrates.

*Residential Homes for Elderly People and People with a Physical Handicap in England and Wales*

|  | 1981 | 1990 | % change |
|---|---|---|---|
| Local Authority | 122,691 | 112,626 | −8.2% |
| Voluntary | 38,082 | 36,145 | −5.1% |
| Commercial | 40,737 | 153,229 | +276% |

(*Source:* Adapted from Darton, 1993)

Most of this growth had been financed from the state through social security payments to enable people to purchase care, which was encouraged from the early days of the Thatcher government onwards. These payments had increased from £10 million in 1979 to more than £1,000 million by 1989 (Local Government Information Unit, 1990). Walker (1989, 1993) argues that much of this was due to a deliberate policy by the Thatcher government to restrict local authority expenditure and encourage the private sector. The Audit Commission was concerned not only that this unsupervised policy encouraged costly residential care which might otherwise be more cheaply provided, but also that the money might be better spent on domiciliary care in people's homes to obviate the need for admission to homes. The Griffiths Report and the 1990 reforms which followed it were based on the premise that shifting the social security budget to local authorities as part of the revenue support grant would enable them to provide a rationally based system which would end the 'perverse bias' in favour of residential care, and also ensure better value for money.

Let us now therefore focus directly on the 1990 community care reforms, to compare their claimed and likely effects.

# Chapter 4
# The Griffiths reforms –
# a needs-based system
# at last?

The proposals in the Government's White Paper in 1989, *Caring for People*, which were embodied in the NHS and Community Care Act of 1990, laid down clear objectives against which its policies could be evaluated. The changes, it said, are intended to enable people to live as normal a life as possible in their own homes or in a homely environment in the local community.

As we shall see towards the end of this book, this objective raises enormous philosophical and practical questions about the kind of 'normal life' which should be made available as a social right. However as a starting point it marks a radical and welcome departure in social policy which in principle endorses the philosophy of 'normalisation', proclaiming that the needs, wishes, and interests of users to be the central public objective of community care. The key question of course is how this is to be realised in practice, an issue which certainly vexed the government, who, concerned at the financial implications, immediately delayed implementation of the key planning and financial aspects of the legislation beyond the original planned date of April 1991. Only since April 1993 has the Act been fully operational.

The centrepiece of the Griffiths system as enshrined in the 1990 Act, was a needs-based system of assessment through individualised 'case management', in which appropriate 'packages of care' in the community will be devised with the agreement of users and carers, with an appeal mechanism for disputes.

Where people enter into residential care, they will be entitled to a home of their choice. A 'key worker' system will ensure that people are not discharged from hospital unless care in the community is available. Overall responsibility for community care is to be given to local government, as the 'lead authority' and most appropriate agency for providing social care, and also presumably because local democracy would be a means of ensuring greater responsiveness to users' needs. District health authorities and Family Health Service Authorities (FHSA) are to retain responsibility for community health provision. One of the most novel and progressive aspects of the proposed reforms is the requirement to plan local provision through a production of local

## Main provisions of 1990 Community Care Act

- Local Authorities to have 'lead responsibility' for community care
- Transfer of social security element of residential care to local authorities starting in April 1993, with 85 percent to be spent on purchasing residential and domiciliary services from the private sector
- Local Authorities to undertake 'needs assessment' for new clients and design 'packages of care' through a system of 'case management', in consultation with users, and in collaboration with medical, nursing and other interests
- Local Authorities to assess ability to meet 'full economic cost' of residential care, and encouraged to extend charges for other services
- Existing clients to retain right to social security support for residential care
- Local Authorities to consult widely and draw up clear Community Care Plans consistent with local health authority plans
- Local Authorities to establish clear procedures for dealing with complaints and comments from users
- Local Authorities encouraged to split purchaser and provider functions, and experiment with contracting for care - but no formal internal market on NHS lines established
- Local Authorities to set up 'arms length' Inspection and Registration units to monitor standards in their own and independent residential care homes
- Health Authorities to retain significant responsibility for community care of people suffering from mental illness, funded in part by a Specific Grant from central government
- Department of Health's Social Services Inspectorate to monitor local authority social care provision from above and advise the Secretary of State accordingly
- Secretary of State invested with wide powers to give guidance and issue directions
- Means to be developed to shift resources more easily across the health and social care divide

Community Care Plans either independently or in conjunction with local health authorities. Either way, there was a requirement to consult widely and involve users in the production of local Community Care Plans from April 1992. The resources to fund this new system involved some transitional support, but mainly in a staged way. The residential care element of social security is being ringfenced and transferred to local authorities between 1993-96, after which it will become part of their Standard Spending Assessment. The aim of this is to end 'perverse incentives' to residential care embodied in the former system. The hope is that local authorities will increasingly use the money to fund domiciliary, day and respite support for people to continue living in their homes, leading to a shift away from long term residential care. Most criticism of government policy is less about this overall aim, than whether it has provided sufficient resources to bring this about, as well as the precise means it has laid down, involving the continued shift to a 'mixed (in fact increasingly privatised) economy of care'.

The Griffiths Report was seen as a considerable boost to the standing of local government, whose powers had been progressively eroded in the 1980s by a vengeful Tory government not only concerned to contain expenditure and encourage private provision, but determined to restrict the activities of left-wing Labour councils. However Griffiths made clear that though local authorities would plan community care, and supervise standards by administering 'arm's length' Inspection Units and complaints systems, their prime role would be as 'enablers' rather than 'providers' of care and 'maximum use' would be made of the independent sector. In theory this would encourage the emergence of an even-handed 'mixed economy of care', the creation of a quasi-market in which prospective providers in the public, commercial and voluntary sectors would compete to offer cost effective and quality residential or domiciliary care, while at the same time widening the choices available to users.

The government largely accepted Sir Roy Griffiths' recommendations in the 1989 White Paper, *Caring for People*, which foreshadowed the 1990 Act. They initially rejected, but have since accepted, his proposal that the social security funds transferred be ring-fenced temporarily to ensure that they were spent on community care. They have, however, not acted on his proposal that a Minister for Community Care be appointed to ensure integration and advocacy at national level.

## Overdue Recognition for Carers?

A prominent feature of the Griffiths Report was the acknowledgement of the role that carers play in community care. Although this was stated within the context of a model ideologically committed to care in the community, there was an explicit acknowledgement of the central role of carers as producers of community care, whose views, and needs for support and respite services, and training to develop skills, needed to be given a promi-

## A needs-led service?

The following imaginary dialogue between a provider and user was reported in the 9 April issue of *Community Care*.

**Social Worker:** You need an assessment, you know. You are a valued member of society. We have a needs-led service. We can help you, we want you to lead the life of your choice. With dignity and freedom from want. Go on let me assess you please.

**Woman:** Oh all right then, if you think it would help.

**Social Worker:** Well Mrs Bloggs following my in-depth assessment I can now tell you that you need home care, meals-on-wheels and day care daily, your house completely refurbished and cleaned out, your garden tidied up, your hair cutting, and your toenails as well, plus a sheltered bungalow with a sea view. You could also use a two-week holiday in Barbados, plus someone to open your door, cater for visitors, wash and dress you.

**Woman:** Oh really, that's very nice. What a nice assessing-type person you are. I really like you and trust you now. When will you get me all of those things then?

**Social Worker:** Ah well, you see Mrs Bloggs, we won't be able to get you all of it. We should be able to do a home help, say for half-an-hour a week. We have no money you see, but I will tell our manager what you needed and couldn't have. I will call again for a chat.

nent place in planning and provision. Official policy had previously assumed, in line with patriarchal ideology, that caring could just be assumed by women as 'a labour of love' (Graham, 1983).

This recognition is of course double-edged, analogous in many ways to the status attached by Beveridge in 1942 to the housewife, which in practice reinforced the notion of housework as women's work. In a similar way Griffiths and *Caring for People* are gender blind to the fact that the majority of carers are women, and therefore have no proposals for securing a more equitable social division of care between men and women, nor do they say anything about the needs of male carers for that matter. The aims of the White Paper are to ensure that fewer people go into residential care, and the only way it can do this is to ensure that carers do the work, albeit with more gestures toward providing support and training than in the past. Since, as we shall see, limited resources will require local authorities to concentrate such help on the most dependent and/or impoverished people, this will mean increased amounts of informal care provided by carers of very dependent people and those with a more moderate need for support.

Carers remain a largely hidden army, and little is publicly known about them and those they service. What we do know, as Jane King (1989) puts it, is that informal carers 'provide more community care than the statutory, private and voluntary sectors put together'. This contribution is set to increase even more in the future. The General Household Survey of the Office of Population Census and Surveys (OPCS) indicated that in 1985 there were nearly seven million carers of which 3.7 million carried the main caring responsibility, and 1.4 million who put in more than 20 hours a week (Green, 1988). As Gillian Parker's research review points out: 'Once one carer has been identified as the main carer other relatives withdraw' (G Parker, 1990). The 1985 survey found that more carers were women than men, though there were significant numbers of male carers, particularly among carers aged over 65. Carers often combined caring with other paid and unpaid responsibilities. More than half of carers suffered themselves from health problems which limited their activities (as quoted by Brotchie and Mills, 1991). As Graham (1993) points out, this necessitates recognition that 'receivers' and 'givers' are not rigid, mutually-exclusive groups. Many women with disabilities are heavily involved in both self-care and in servicing other family members (p. 127).

The need for care is bound to increase with the increase in the numbers of older people over the next two decades.

Caring is hard work, not just in the sense that it can often be physically taxing, but also skilled and emotionally demanding (Graham, 1983; James, 1992/3). Most often, as we have seen, these demands reinforce familial obligations on women. However, even in such circumstances relationships between carer and cared for often establish changed relations of dependency, which become highly emotionally charged for both sides of the encounter, for example, between mothers and daughters (Morris, 1991). While a significant number of carers are men, they are more likely to be caring for wives and rarely for elderly parents. In addition, there is greater recognition by agencies of the 'incongruous' position of male carers, and greater preparedness by outside agencies to offer support (Arber and Gilbert, 1989). Nevertheless, there is is considerable diversity of relations of care that are obscured by stereotypical views of it as a woman's role (Graham, 1993). For example, one hidden aspect of caring which highlights these issues, that has recently come to light in research by Aldridge and Becker (1993), is the extent to which children and young people are often primary or significant carers. Not only did they find there to be a heightened social tension between the 'traditional role of the child who needs love, support and to be taken care of… and the role of young carer where the child is the guardian of their own parent's welfare' (p vii). They also found that professionals were even less likely than normal to acknowledge their responsible and expert role as carers, and consult with them over service provision.

Caring is also costly to those concerned and to society at large. If a full social accounting system is used, then the view that a transfer of care from the public sector (including the publicly funded 'independent' sector) is 'cost effective' or even 'saves money' is wildly inaccurate. Research into these costs has only recently been initiated (Parker, 1990, Ch3). A study by Caroline Glendinning (1992) showed that money worries figured highly in the concerns of carers. Caring responsibilities involved one off capital costs such as housing alterations and special aids, as well as regular extra household expenditure on such items as heating, laundry, special diets, and repairs. At the same time her research showed that caring severely curtailed employment opportunities for those of working age, with many having to stop work altogether. Glendinning suggests that not only must more support be provided by statutory services, but employment practices must also change to enable caring and employment to be combined, alongside improvements to support through the benefits system.

The TUC's Charter for Carers, produced in 1991 in partnership with the Carers National Association, draws attention to the economic costs to society of inflexible and discriminatory employment practices, and reinforces arguments that caring is skilled as well as physically demanding and emotionally taxing. It now throws the weight of the trade union movement behind the demand for a new deal for carers, including access to flexible working packages, protection of pay, training and other benefits, and a statutory right to special leave. What is also significant about the Charter, in the light of persuasive arguments that the left and the feminist movement have sometimes prioritised the needs of carers over users (eg by Morris, 1991/2), is the emphasis in the Charter on the right of 'all frail elderly and disabled people... to the support of professional carers'. This involves an overdue recognition of the fact that informal care can be an inappropriate imposition on users as well as carers – an issue which has profound implications for the funding and organisation of community care. Although research shows that many people prefer to be cared for by relatives, a significant number of users feel that the option of paid care offers more choice and control (Qureshi, 1990; Morris, 1991).

This is evidence of extensive and pressing need which cannot be met by simply shuffling around a few financial resources from social security to a revamped local government system of community care. Responding to it requires a wideranging review of the relationship of caring to the wider social institutions of the family, state and workplace. At best therefore, Griffiths and the White Paper of 1989 which followed it represented only a token gesture towards a new deal for carers. In any case times have now changed. Griffiths was a product of the mid-80s concern with the 'demographic time bomb', the concern that in future 'producers' (that is, paid workers) would outnumber 'non-producers'. The context for this was the assumed success of the so-called British economic miracle, which implied that all hands were now required on deck, including women, as paid workers.

Hence the renewed – if superficial – emphasis on equal opportunities at work, factory nurseries, the Project 2000 reform of nurse education and, in this context, an emphasis on social provision to enable more unpaid carers to combine their responsibilities with paid work. In the context of the 1990s economic depression and public expenditure crisis, this social project has now run into the sand. This may well be one reason why, as Hadley (1992) notes, official concern about the position of carers has recently subsided.

## Sensitivity to the Needs of Black People?

Griffiths and the White Paper made even more muted token gestures in the direction of the community care needs of black and Asian people, even though, as Bandana Ahmed, Director of the National Institute of Social Work put it, 'every section of the White Paper has implications for the black community' (Redding, 1989). A number of commentators have expressed concern that black people's interests will as a result often be sidelined by the community care reforms (Langan, 1990; Local Government Information Unit, 1992).

There is mounting evidence which suggests that black people's needs are not being met by existing services. They are likely to face over-intervention by health and social services in some areas, often with custodial effect. Especially in mental health services, they are more likely than white people to be perceived as potentially threatening. This is reflected in an over-diagnosis of psychotic disorders, particularly schizophrenia, necessitating compulsory admission, compared to white people. Where diagnosed as suffering from a psychotic disorder, they are more likely than white people to be sentenced to prison than sent to a hospital. In mental hospitals they are more likely to receive custodial and 'physical' forms of care (Tonkin, 1987; Fernando, 1991; Lowe, 1992; Skellington and Morris, 1992).

Where intervention cannot be justified on the grounds of presumed threat, there is a converse tendency for black people's health needs to be neglected compared to those of white people. They are less likely to be diagnosed as suffering from 'psychoneuroses' and depression (Skellington and Morris, 1992, Chapter 5), with Asian women's needs for mental health services perhaps most neglected of all (Jervis, 1986). A report by the Black Mental Health Group based on users and carers in Lewisham confirmed the picture of a strong police involvement in admissions, heavy drug use on patients and even violence by staff, and insensitivity to the needs of black carers. The group calls not just for more training of white workers, but for black mental health services staffed by black workers (Black Mental Health Group, 1992).

A similar pattern emerges in health and social services provision as a whole (Connelly, 1988). As Skellington and Morris (1992) put it:

The evidence suggests that black and minority ethnic groups are under-represented as clients receiving the preventive and supportive elements of social services provision, but over-represented in those aspects of social services activity which involve social control functions and/or institutionalisation (p.87).

Thus disproportionate numbers of black children are taken into care by local authorities. Research by Barn (1990) has indicated that this was largely due on the one hand to economic and social circumstances, which could alternatively have been tackled by preventive measures, and compounded by the 'pathologising' attitudes of social workers and other agencies involved.

Ironically, while racist and deeply embedded notions about the inadequacy of black families lead to intervention in families with children, contradictory and equally unfounded assumptions about the ability of black families to provide support for elders is one factor underlying a failure to provide black people with their fair share of available community care services. According to the Carer's Unit of the Kings Fund Centre:

Black carers are more likely to be seen as able to look after their own. Black carers and those they care for are less likely to use community services despite little evidence that they have less need. Black carers tend not to use respite care services for a break because most services do not cater properly for the person needing care. Most information on services is not available in languages which would make it accessible to all Black carers (Kings Fund Centre, 1992).

As with gender stereotyping, racial stereotyping in community care obscures considerable diversity both among and between Asian and African-Caribbean people. For example:

Asian peoples come from a variety of countries and cultures, representing different dialects, languages, histories and customs. These differences have meant that not all Asian carers in this country have the same experiences and needs (Gunaratnum, 1993, p. 114).

One effect of this diversity is that the extent to which Asian people have access to an extended family network to provide care has been exaggerated.

Alongside this emphasis on the stereotypical strengths of family structures is a failure to take account of the effects of discrimination and socioeconomic disadvantage on use of services. These factors, rather than the supposed availability of community support, may better explain why, for example, black people are particularly under-represented as users of residential care. In addition, little account is generally taken of how socioeconomic disadvantage as reflected in employment, income and residence adversely affects the ability of black people to provide informal care (Local Government Information Unit, 1992).

All this does not provide much encouragement for the view that black people will get a fairer share of the cash-limited community care resources being transferred to local authority social services departments from April 1993. The preliminary findings of a Department of Health-funded study conducted by the Age Concern Institute of Gerontology in areas with significant black and minority ethnic populations, indicate that while (only) three-quarters of social services departments made some efforts to meet dietary needs through meals-on-wheels services, their record on addressing black people's specific needs in domiciliary and residential care was very under-developed. For example, half had no specific interpreting provision and one-third no specific home help provision. A similar picture emerged in health authorities, with three-quarters making provision for special diets, but a much smaller number having a policy covering a broad range of needs. There was often an absence of even basic types of provision: half neither employed nor funded any interpreters! (Askham and Pharoah, 1992).

Thus personal racism is compounded by institutionally racist structures which fail to take account of the difficulties that black and ethnic minority people face in asserting their needs and do not recognise, let alone address, the social structural causes of racial disadvantage (see Skellington and Morris, 1992; Amin and Oppenheim, 1992). This inability of health and social services departments to respond to the needs of black users is also closely related to their failure over many years to tackle personal and institutional racism in their employment structures, a point raised by many commentators, including NUPE (Doyal, Hunt and Mellor, 1981; Bhat, Carr-Hill and Ohri, 1988; NUPE, 1990a, Chapter 6; Skellington and Morris, 1992).

All this raises major issues of concern which needed more than the 1989 White Paper's token encouragement to do more. Without a stronger lead from central government there is no particular reason to believe that contracting and the shift to the market will deliver greater sensitivity to black users' needs, given the poor records of health and local authorities in the past. There is every reason to fear that, despite the efforts of some authorities, the present unfair situation will not improve and could even get worse. Already there are suggestions that recession and financial capping are slowing down the recruitment, training and career advancement of black staff. In addition fewer Labour local authorities are now likely to make concerted efforts to address racism than in the past, out of a desire to shrug off a 'loony left' image (Murray, 1992). The cutting back of grants to, and shift to 'contract culture', among voluntary organisations (see below) is also likely to have implications for the responsiveness of community care services to black users and particularly their political independence from the state (Institute of Race Relations, 1993).

## All Power to the Users?

The tendency to greatly exaggerate the progressive aspects of the reforms is also a feature of the token gestures towards user-involvement. The 1989 White Paper talks only vaguely about giving people 'an individual say' in the services they receive, and has no explicit mechanisms for ensuring that this takes place. There are no nationally defined rights to provision, as for example established in however limited a way by the Citizen's Charter in other forms of public provision. As Don Redding (1989) points out, the emphasis is on monitoring from above by the Department of the Environment, and advocacy of a form of case management which in practice is more likely to encourage rationing than empowerment of users. People will be assessed against a known background of what services are available, and determining ability to pay will be a central part of the process of case management.

No doubt well-resourced and decentralised case (now called 'care') management can be a means of improving services by allowing social workers and other care staff to provide flexible forms of support for people in their own homes, as in the original Kent scheme (Challis and Davies, 1986; Challis et al, 1993). However its narrow focus on discrete services within fixed budgets has led some to argue that it can also tend to screen out more political approaches to social work and community care concerned to secure collective social change (Baldock, 1989). Under the original Kent care management scheme, social workers were free to purchase from the commercial or voluntary sectors, a practice which must have commended it to the government as well as the fact that significant savings were made compared with institutional care. Much of the social worker's responsibility under care management will focus on investigating the means available without resort to increasingly scarce public provision including personal resources and voluntary sector provision. Contracting through 'service specification' of standards for given costs undoubtedly gives more power to the lead authority but not necessarily to the individual user. Yet though it might sometimes expand choice and ensure improved quality, it has limited use as a means of empowering users to ensure services are delivered in accordance with their wishes. At the very least it needs to be backed up by user involvement in checking standards of service by carrying out user inspections. Another proposal which has come out of the disability movement, but which needs careful thought – not least because it has the support of right-wing think tanks – is the proposal that individual users should receive money grants or vouchers which they could spend on services as they wish. Money payments for packages of care under the Act will not be paid to individuals. Such money could be used to enabled carers to choose between paid work and paid care and would be set at a more realistic 'wage' level than available through attendance allowances. Direct payment could empower users to employ someone as a personal carer, something which has been available to to people with physical disabilities through the Independent Living Fund set up in 1986 (and now being phased out). These issues pose difficult and complex issues for socialists and trade unionists, in balancing the needs of paid workers and users, and in deciding on the extent to which public authorities should be intervene in such employment relationships to protect either or both parties. There are no easy answers, but at the very least the onus is on public service trade unionists to show that means are available through public provision that give users and carers real choices and command over resources.

It is regrettable that schemes of service delivery aimed at increasing accountability to service users, such as in Birmingham and Leeds, and the All Wales Strategy for Mental Handicap, have not had a greater influence on the community care reforms. This is not to over-romanticise such schemes. A review of the All-Wales Strategy found that users wanted a greater say in services than were generally offered them (Titterton, 1993). An evaluation of the Birmingham Community Care Special Action Project (BCCSAP) found that service providers felt that users' interests had achieved a higher profile in decision making, but this view was not shared by users (Barnes, 1993, p. 56).

As Croft and Beresford (1990) point out, involvement can mean forms of opinion research or consultation which do not give users a real say. They also distinguish between individual involvement at case level, in the running of services, and in planning their overall development. In their view, self-advocacy of users is a necessary requirement at all three levels (quoted by John Black, 1992). Clarke and Stewart (1992) make the important point that there is a need to distinguish between empowering people individually as either customers or citizens, or collectively as a community. They suggest that unless the latter means of empowerment is given sufficient emphasis, including the provision of adequate resources, individual empowerment may often be at the expense of some other person.

In principle the community care reforms have raised the possibility of a needs-based system, in which users have a powerful voice in determining their own needs, but can not deliver this in practice. This is partly because of shortfalls in resources but also because, as we have seen, the systems of contracting adopted are unlikely to offer users or carers much individual control over services. As Hunter (1993) observes, needs assessment may well create a paternalistic system in which people have less real say than when they had a right to residential care under the previous social security based system. Perhaps there will be more possibilities for collective empowerment through the requirement that local authorities and health authorities seek to develop local community care plans through wide consultation with local people. In principle, this is something which trade unionists and socialists would support. In the past local councils have been rather remote and bureaucratic, and the community care reforms offer the prospect of developing a decentralised model of 'popular planning for social need'. Since such local plans only began to appear in 1992, and vary considerably in style and content it is rather early to make definitive conclusions, though one or tentative observations can be made. First, as NALGO (1993) has pointed out many plans appear to be over-optimistic about what services will be provided and how they will be delivered, and fail to confront openly the fact that harsh decisions will need to be taken. This observation is confirmed in research undertaken by Gerard Wistow and his colleagues (1993a; 1993b), whose analysis of the first batch of plans produced in April 1992 showed that most contained few costed elements, let alone specified arrangements for monitoring and review. Second, their research indicates that many authorities have largely ignored the requirement to consult widely with local people, or have only done so in a token fashion. These problems, they argue, are compounded by the lack of planning experience of local authorities.

There is thus no doubt that the reforms have given some encouragement to the development of schemes of empowerment, though these are often being introduced by progressive authorities, professionals and user groups despite, rather than because of, the community care reforms. Yet although there are those on the left who enthuse about the opportunities that service contracting presents for democratisation of services (see, for example, Pfieffer and Coote, 1991), the greatest emphasis is likely to be on individual 'customer' empowerment in a strictly controlled budgetary system which facilitates the privatisation of services. Resource constraints will intensify competition among groups of users. How this will work out in practice is not yet clear. One view, expressed by NALGO (1993), is that most priority will be given in the first instance to services for older people, since the government has itself acknowledged that in the first year the bias towards residential care, which primarily provides for older people, will continue. As this bias diminishes, it might well be the case that more articulate groups of users are able to corner a bigger share of the cake.

All this presumes of course that users will be influential. In practice care management may be implemented either as a new form of social work professionalism based on mystification of casework skills, or as a more bureaucratic and 'deskilled' system based on block contracts determined at a high level in the structure. Either system is likely to only offer token involvement to users. As NALGO (1990b) puts it:

Real involvement of users in planning requires fundamental changes in local authority processes.

This view is confirmed by radical commentators on user-empowerment within community care, who draw attention to the need to develop specific strategies backed up by resources to make it possible. As Alan Walker (1993) puts it:

> User involvement must be built in to the structure and operation of Social Service Departments and not bolted on. In the absence of firm and specific guidelines on how to achieve this, one cannot be too optimistic that it will generally be a strong feature of the new pattern of community care provision, though some progressive Labour Councils are doing their best to develop user and carer empowerment.

## The Coercive Shift to Privatisation and Commodification

Though there are only vague gestures towards meeting the needs of users and carers, there is much more of a sustained policy to enforce privatisation, or what Alan Walker has called the 'residualisation' of care (1989, 1993). This is dressed up as an even-handed and pluralistic mixed economy of care, but the 1989 White Paper made it clear that local authorities are 'to make maximum possible use of private and voluntary providers, and so increase the available range of options and widen consumer choice' (paragraph 1.11). In practice contracting is to be weighted heavily against the public sector. NALGO (1990a) made the point that a mixed economy involving the public, commercial and voluntary sectors was already in existence when Sir Roy drafted his report. Local authorities were already discriminated against under the existing system as, unlike the private and voluntary sectors, they were not subsidised through social security payments on top of Income Support (known officially as Income Support for People in Registered Residential Care Homes and Nursing Homes), or through Housing Benefit and Attendance Allowance. Although, unlike the NHS, local authorities will not be required to set up an internal market, they will be expected to resort to the private and voluntary sectors. Most commentators agree that determination to enforce this, rather than concern that quality standards are maintained, is the main reason why the Department of the Environment has been given reserve powers to intervene.

This coercive shift to privatisation will be enforced by resources being transferred across from the social security budget. The securing of £539 million for local authorities in England from April 1993, the date when the Community Care Act came into full effect, has been represented as a triumph against the Treasury by the Minister of Health, Virginia Bottomley. However it falls a long way short of the amounts that local authorities in England, Scotland and Wales had themselves projected as necessary to assume their new responsibilities (though any estimate of 'need' is uncertain given lack of precise knowledge). And there are some additional catches.

• Although the government has finally decided that transferred money should be temporarily ring-fenced, this will not apply to other money for social services obtained through the revenue support grant. Given the intense pressures that many councils are under as a result of the Council Tax settlement from central government, and the traditional bias against care noted earlier, overall cuts in social services expenditure on community care will occur in many areas, and many users will pay increased means-tested charges for what services remain (George, 1992).

• Eighty five per cent of the £539 million allocated for England must be spent in the 'independent' sector, in other words all of the £399 million which is being transferred from social security in 1993-4. And the same rules will apply in subsequent years. As we have seen, in the past people received a guaranteed amount from social security to cover the costs of residential care, albeit increasingly inadequate – according to the Registered Nursing Homes Association some £30-50 a week below cost. In future new applicants will receive whatever their local authority decides they need on top of normal Income Support, and Attendance Allowance will not be available for local authority assisted places in the voluntary and commercial sector (NALGO, 1990a).

• Local authorities must continue to find the full cost of any residential care they provide, as the £45 a week Income Support for Residential Care will not be payable to residents in local authority homes. All this will create a mixed economy of care stacked in favour of the private and voluntary sectors. It will also deny individuals the choice to be cared for within the public sector.

In other words rather than extending rights to community care, the Act will erode them. Users and carers will increasingly be forced to spend their savings or sell their houses to pay for domiciliary and residential care (George, 1992; Lister, 1992). This has already been a clear trend, particularly in relation to Alzheimer's Disease and other forms of dementing illness whose incidence increases dramatically with age, to the extent that, according to the government's Health of the Nation White Paper, twenty per cent of people over eighty suffer from its effects. This was highlighted in a Report by the Alzheimer's Disease Society (1993) which showed that financial difficulties add considerably to the strains of carers who may put in more than eighty hours a week looking after relatives. The alternative to home care is costly nursing homes, which as Alasdair Palmer (1993) explains, put particular financial pressures on older women who rely on their husbands' occupational pension:

> If a woman's husband falls victim to dementia, all of that pension will be sequestered to pay for his treatment. With nursing homes costing as much as £2,000 a month, most pensions will be gobbled up immediately. The next target is savings. Anything above £8,000 can be taken.

The recouping of costs in this way goes back to 1984, and is perhaps one of the most dramatic examples of 'dumping' on to relatives and the private sector through community care, which is exacerbated rather than eased by the 1990 Community Care Act. Within the new streamlined health service which emerged in the 1980s there has been increasing pressure on removing patients with dementing illness from NHS beds so that the 'throughput' of acutely ill patients could be raised and performance 'improved'. Since that time increasingly dehumanised language, such as 'bed-blocking', has been used to delegitimise the use of NHS beds for long term care. One consultant geriatrician has even recently suggested that a NHS bed should only be 'free' (in fact we pay for it through taxation) for three months, after which those who could afford it would be charged £500 a week (Kellett, 1993)!

It is clear, now that the full financial details have emerged, that the dominant effects will be less to extend social rights and choice, and primarily to place the lid on community care expenditure, by abolishing the 'demand-led' and institutionally-biased system which had grown up under social security funding. In its place a strictly cash-limited and means tested system has been established, which will be policed by local authorities. Portrayed as decentralisation in action to enable services to be tailored to local people's needs, many suspect that the aim is to shift the blame for the inevitable disappointment and disillusionment with the promises of *Caring for People* and the 1990 Act onto local authorities (Local Government Information Unit, 1990a). When public dissatisfaction mounts, central government may be 'forced' to intervene, and seek to discredit the standing of local authorities with their local populations.

In the run up to April 1993, the date when the Community Care Act came into full effect, many homes and other services had already been privatised, as the results of a survey by the Public Services Privatisation Research Unit (1993), of which UNISON are a major sponsor, have shown. The Unit's *Report on Community Care* shows that financial pressures due to capping, together with the shift to contracting involved in the community care legislation, are confirming the view of Alan Walker (1993) that a process of 'residualisation' of local authority care is occurring. This is also reflected in the actual and projected policies of health authorities and trusts. The clearest pattern that seems to be emerging is the closure of many local authority homes for older people, often as a result of expenditure capping pressures. A significant amount of transfer to the voluntary sector is occurring, in which housing associations figure prominently in residential care for older people. There are also the beginnings of a private market in domiciliary and day care, which can be expected to increase with the progressive transfer of social security monies after April 1993. Local authorities are increasingly making use of management consultants such as Cooper and Lybrand to advise them on how to implement these approaches. The Report cites many examples, among the most dramatic being South Glamorgan, which to avoid capping pressures closed seven homes and transferred eight to Corlan Housing Association, and Bromley which has contracted out its entire residential service for older people. As the Report states, apart from the effects of these changes on the staff concerned, groups of users who often require stability and continuity in care, are being subjected to considerable changes to their services in a climate of diminishing funds.

Charges for community care services, encouraged by the 1989 White Paper, are becoming widespread and are increasing, as also is means testing (George, 1992). The pressure on resources may well force councils to give priority to residential care of the most dependent, rather than preventive domiciliary provision for the many, thus defeating one of the central aims of the reforms (Hinchcliffe, 1992). Faced with these economic pressures and increasing demands for services, local authorities will thus be forced to institute further cuts or charges in domiciliary services and other essential services such as housing.

Much of the coercive shift to privatisation has been justified on the grounds that the commercial sector will offer more choice and sensitivity to individual needs. As Alan Walker (1989) points out, this is based on ideology rather than evidence, which indicates that on the whole the commercial sector carefully selects clients according to mental and physical disability, and often turns away those whom it regards as difficult to provide care for. This 'residualisation' process will be accelerated by the Act, with the local government sector increasingly taking the most frail and mentally distressed older people, reinforcing stigma and marginality. As the review by Roy Parker (1990b) concludes, most of what the private sector does is hidden from view, partly by the fragmentation of the services, and by inadequacies in the registration system set up in 1984 and not redressed by the 'arm's length' local authority Inspection Units being now established by the 1990 Act. Needless to say this lack of knowledge, as in other areas of health and social policy, does not prevent the government from pressing ahead regardless. Privatisation is not only taking place in residential but also in domiciliary care. Age Concern has voiced alarm that the service may disappear altogether from local authorities and be undertaken in future by private agencies, with no checks on the service and the people such agencies provide (Fry, 1992).

Whether or not services are privatised, they will become 'commodified', even if they continue to be provided within the public sector. The increasing separation between purchasing and providing functions, and the shift to contract culture within local authorities will facilitate this by creating a separation within formerly professionally oriented social services departments, between those who plan and manage and those who deliver services (Geldert, 1993). Lower down the line another set of hierarchical relationships are being erected through a separation between those who assess individual needs and those whose job it will be to provide for them. Such a top heavy system will commodify services in the sense that they will tend to be 'prepackaged' packages of care, rather than holistic and tailored to individual needs by front line workers in partnership with users and carers. Services are being commodified in this way in order to facilitate privatisation, rationing and means testing. So rather than being genuinely sensitive to individual needs, the new community care offers the prospect of restricted access to increasingly standardised 'products'. This 'Mc-Donaldisation' of community care is part of a wider societal process of rationalisation based on Taylorist principles (Ritzer, 1993).

The populist justification of this system is that managerial control of previously bureaucratic and professionally driven services is necessary to break the producer-led system of the past so that users can be empowered. The underlying doctrine behind this, as David Hunter (1993) has argued, is 'new public service management', particularly associated with Sir Roy Griffiths, which sees markets and 'quasi markets', facilitated by the spread of information technology, as giving management freedom to manage and innovate. However there are doubts about whether this new system will live up to expectations. Managers and needs assessment staff will contract on behalf of users in this emerging system and commodified care will as a result not be compatible with true accountability to users. As Hunter also argues, contracting based on market principles rather than need is likely to fail through not taking account of the complexity of assessing 'performance' in public services. In the meantime the interests of users are more likely to be served by the continuing commitment of staff to a more traditional 'public service' ethic.

Sir Roy Griffiths had claimed that 'community care is a poor relation:

everybody's distant relative and nobody's baby' (paragraph 9). His hope and expectation was that giving 'parental' rights to local authorities might lead to a new era for users of community care. Yet as we have seen, strict central government financial controls and encouragement to privatisation means that local authorities will at best be foster parents, too starved of resources to nurse community care to maturity. This all means that in practice social rights to provision and involvement will be more rhetorical than real, and even government ministers and agencies are now seeking to play down public expectations of the reforms. A report by the Audit Commission (1992) has warned that unless the changes are scheduled carefully, local authorities 'could be overwhelmed' given their existing financial circumstances and the failure to transfer cash along with the responsibilities shifted across from health.

The biggest losers in all this will be women – women who as the majority of users find their access to services rationed or have to pay for it themselves; carers who may find that they will be expected to shoulder more care to prevent admission to expensive residential care; and paid workers who face increased pressures to deliver more with less, or risk losing their jobs as services are privatised (Local Government Information Unit, 1990b; NALGO, 1990a). The shift to contracting-out under case management will reinforce the already pronounced class, gender and 'race' inequalities among paid providers, with a smaller number of 'core' professionalised case workers and a growing number of exploited workers on the privatised 'periphery' where most care will be carried out. Rather than promising a new era, this will also reinforce existing healthism, devaluation of care, and stigmatisation of recipients and providers whether paid or unpaid.

## A New Role for the Voluntary Sector

There is good foundation for the fears expressed in *Community Care: Which Way Forward?*, COHSE's commentary on the reforms prior to the 1990 Act, and echoed by Langan (1990), that voluntary sector organisations will have to adopt an increasingly commercial ethos and approach if they are to survive in the market-oriented contracting environment, diminishing their campaigning and innovative role. This will of course also affect the way they treat their staff. NALGO (1993) argued that:

> One of the main reasons why the voluntary sector can provide a cheap service is the poor wages, conditions and job security given to staff.

If this occurs, rather than encouraging pluralism, the reforms will remould voluntary organisations. I described earlier how in a previous era philanthropic organisations were generally anti-state and concentrated on various forms of 'rescue work'. The voluntary sector is very diverse, but on the whole organisations are now largely supportive of the welfare state, and have increasingly adopted a campaigning style and emphasised empowerment of users. A shift to a managerialist-consumerism model may help in fact to 're-colonise' voluntary organisations and make them adopt more socially conformist approaches, a concern increasingly being voiced within the voluntary movement (Hedley and Smith, 1991). This is reinforced by pressure from the Charity Commissioner to restrain voluntary organisations from becoming 'political'. Concern has also been expressed that the bureaucracy associated with contracting for services, as compared to bidding for grants as in the past, will militate against user involvement and necessitate a more hierarchical approach by voluntary organisations (Gosling, 1992).

This is a point that has already been made about contracting, that rather than empowering users it is something which often goes on above their heads, and which sets standards and levels of provision which have to be taken into account when individual needs are assessed. In this scenario, though contracting has the positive effect of making standards explicit, it also facilitates rationing of services. As far as voluntary organisations are concerned, this is likely to lead to intensified and unseemly rivalry among voluntary organisations for the cash limited pot of transferred social security money as the government withdraws from grant-aided funding (Eaton, 1993).

Contracting has many forms, and although it may sometimes facilitate choice, the parameters of choice have been set by the negotiations between purchasers and providers. Contracts can therefore militate against choice because they are typically bargains struck on behalf of users rather than with their direct involvement (North, 1993). With the emphasis so much centred on cost, the likelihood is that economies of scale will encourage larger rather than smaller commercial and voluntary organisations. This will tend to discriminate against the smaller, campaigning organisations in the 'self-help' sector, particularly those representing women and black people, who do not have the time or resources to devote to contracting. Since many of the smaller voluntary organisations are those which are locally based, the shift to contracting is therefore likely to inhibit local responsiveness to needs. At the same time as the voluntary sector becomes more bureaucratic, and involved in mainstream provision, it is therefore also likely to become less accessible, innovative and diverse.

In the past there has been mistrust of the voluntary sector by unions on the grounds that volunteers have been substituted for employed workers and used by management to undermine industrial disputes. There is also a tendency for professionals to look down on volunteers as inexpert 'do-gooders' with few skills to contribute. The labour movement has particularly been concerned that the government has been seeking to use the voluntary movement as a battering ram against the welfare state since the 1980s, when notions such as 'active citizenship' were deliberately countered

## Guidelines for relations between volunteers and paid workers in the health and personal social services

### Section 1: General Guidelines

1. Voluntary activity should complement the work of paid staff, not substitute for it
2. The action of volunteers should not threaten the livelihood of paid staff
3. Any change in the level of voluntary activity should be preceded by full consultation between interested parties
4. Agreements on the nature and extent of voluntary activity should be made widely known among intended parties
5. Volunteers should receive full out-of-pocket expenses
6. There should be recognised machinery for the resolution of problems between staff and volunteers
7. Volunteers not involved in industrial action should undertake no more voluntary activity than they would do in the normal situation
8. If volunteers are faced with a picket line which is not prepared to agree that the volunteer workers should cross, the volunteers should not attempt to do so but discuss the situation with their organiser of voluntary service, who should in turn discuss it with union and management officials

### Section 2: Local Agreements

The above guidelines should be taken as a starting point within which local agreements might be constructed, including some or all of the following:

- A statement of intent laying down general principles regarding the involvement of volunteers in the work of the agency or organisation
- Guidelines on avoiding substitution of volunteers for paid workers
- Guidelines on identifying areas of work appropriate for paid staff and appropriate for volunteers
- Guidelines on differentiating between regular volunteers, trainees, secondees, and regular paid workers
- Guidelines on the involvement of volunteers in tendering for and contracting out local government services
- Agreement on the rights and responsibilities of volunteers, including reimbursement of out-of-pocket expenses, provision of insurance, training opportunities, access to decision making, and access to a trade union
- Guidelines on conduct in industrial disputes
- Establishment of a local hotline or other mechanism for quickly resolving difficulties

These 'good practice' Guidelines were drawn up in 1990 under the auspices of the Volunteer Centre UK, by a working party representing statutory authorities, public service trade unions and organisations which involve volunteers. They replace and earlier set produced in 1975.

against 'citizenship rights' to health and welfare services. The encouragement of 'contracting-out' of mainstream services to voluntary agencies is also an attempt to 'residualise' state welfare under the guise of 'welfare pluralism'. As John Major put it plainly enough, 'charities are not the sticking plaster on the welfare state... but the cement that binds our society together' (quoted in Hirst, 1993).

Nevertheless there has been progress towards closer co-operation and mutual respect, which has been helped by such developments as the Guidelines for Volunteers and Paid Workers developed by the Volunteer Centre in conjunction with public service unions and issued in 1990, even though, as NALGO (1993) points out, pay and conditions in the voluntary sector are generally inferior to the public sector. This has been combined with a re-evaluation of the positive innovative role that state-funded voluntary organisations can play in helping to shift welfare in new directions, towards radical, non-hierarchical and 'communitarian' forms of welfare (Heginbotham, 1990). It has been forcefully argued that voluntary organisations based on mutual self-help are consistent with leftist and indeed union principles in ways that warrant an enhanced role for them in publicly funded services (Coote and Deakin, 1991).

It is thus appropriate that the labour movement adopts a different and more positive stance towards state supported voluntary organisations than commercial organisations. Yet that does not necessitate an uncritical and romanticised approach. Diana Leat's wide-ranging survey of voluntary care for older people concluded that:

> The voluntary sector is geographically haphazard in its distribution; its funding is haphazard; its activities are haphazard, and so too are its relationships with local statutory policies and personnel (Leet, 1990, p.275).

Others have argued that that the voluntary sector is not always as democratic and user-sensitive as the 'communitarian' image implies, and that voluntary organisations are ill-equipped to take on the role being thrust on them by the 1990 reforms (Hudson, 1990). Users have often had to struggle within voluntary organisations to make their voice heard, and have often accused leaders of taking a patronising attitude. Voluntary organisations often had an institutional bias in the past, and sociological studies have shown that they often took a 'warehousing' approach (eg Miller and Gwynne, 1971), but see the critique of this study by Morris, 1991, CRS). A recent example of user disenchantment with voluntary organisations is the three-year campaign by People First, a self-advocacy group of people with learning difficulties, to get rid of MENCAP's infamous Little Stephen logo. This included a refusal to board a bus with such a logo and T-shirts with the slogan 'Label jars, not people'. Jenny Morris (1991) claims that charities, in often reinforcing the dominant medical and 'personal tragedy' views of disability, are accomplices to a society which denies disabled people their social rights. She calls for 'organisations of' rather than 'organisations for' disabled people as the only way of countering this tendency. At the same time, there is evidence that voluntary organisations, under challenge from below by users, are to differing degrees changing their structures, policies and ways of working. Her arguments raise important issues for trade unionists as they increasingly target the growing voluntary sector for recruitment. Are they to mainly focus on the pay and conditions of employed workers, or will they ally themselves unreservedly with user movements' campaigns for accountable voluntary organisations and wider social change? This question has particular relevance for UNISON, which has accepted the principle of 'self-organisation' for union members with disabilities, and other oppressed groups.

The coming period will be very difficult for voluntary organisations. In the current climate they face cuts and uncertainties, because they have previously relied on public grants and they will now have to compete for contracts. Already in the run up to the Act, and in the harsh financial climate faced by many urban local authorities, grants to voluntary organisations have been cut by an estimated £42 million, or 7.5% of the total, between 1991-93 (National Council of Voluntary Organisations, 1992).The economic slump has also badly affected donations to charities.

Through contracting, councils and health authorities will be able to off-load their responsibilities, and transfer their own difficult rationing decisions on to voluntary organisations. All this indicates that there needs to be a more strategic look at the relationship between statutory and voluntary health and welfare provision. A start has been made by the Labour Party policy document *Building Bridges* which seeks to ensure value for public money spent, while protecting the campaigning role of voluntary organisations (Ivory, 1992). However, as we have seen, such issues need to be considered in the wider context of social provision as a whole.

## Conclusion: Purely a Con-trick?

This chapter has shown that though articulating principles which could have been the basis for a more radical and 'user centred' approach to community care, the reality is likely to fall a long way short. The cost and market driven ways in which the reforms seek to realise their aims are likely to lead to fewer rather than expanded user rights and choices.

Does this mean that the reforms are merely a 'con-trick' designed to disarm potential opposition? In part, yes, the new alliance which is being constructed between the government and the new managerial elite on the one hand, and users on the other, is designed to place any blame for failure on local authorities and those who work for them. However that is only part of the picture because, as was argued earlier, the criticisms of past services had some substance. More fundamentally, however, there are aspects of the reforms which socialists and trade unionists ought not only to defend but also to extend, particularly their stated emphasis on rights of users to 'a normal life', on assessment of need, and on individual empowerment through flexible and sensitive services, and collective empowerment through involvement in community care planning.

This, and the fact that the reforms are in place and unlikely to be removed in the foreseeable future, create considerable dilemmas for the trade union movement. It is these which the rest of the book seeks to confront. The next chapter examines how the unions which have now merged to form UNISON sought to tackle these difficult issues. The book then moves to try to identify some basic principles for 'good' community care and concludes with a brief discussion of the way forward.

# Chapter 5
# Trade union responses
# to community care

This chapter looks at trade union responses to policy developments in community care since the 1980s, by comparing the experiences of COHSE, NALGO and NUPE, the unions which have now come together to form UNISON, the biggest public services union in Europe with 1.4 million members. I focus more on COHSE than the other two unions, partly because it initially sponsored the research that led to this book. However COHSE, as the main union in mental health services with a stake in hospitals and the health service, as well as public provision, was forced to confront the issue of the shift to community care away from its 'home' territory earlier than other unions. Though its responses to these developments in the 1960s and 1970s were often influenced by a preoccupation to defend workers' interests, an innovative and user oriented approach surfaced in the 1980s which is of interest to UNISON members as a whole and the broader alliance in favour of progressive community care policies. Of course, the shift that COHSE underwent at this time in response to community care, particularly the associated managerialism and growth of private provision, can also be traced through other public service unions, including NALGO and NUPE. As well as leading to new union approaches to public services trade unionism, it was also influential in the creation of UNISON and shaping its philosophy, structures and approach.

## The Tories' End-Game and the trade union response

The origins of this 'new' public service unionism can be traced back to the so-called 'Winter of Discontent' of 1978-79, when low paid public service workers justifiably rebelled against the pay policy of the then Labour government, setting in train events which ushered in the Tories, with whom we have been forced to live for the past fourteen years. Ever since that time the trade union movement has been on the defensive, down if not out. Public service unionism has so far proved relatively resilient, for largely political reasons which they have been able to exploit.

First, there has been no general mandate for an all out assault on the welfare state and it has proved much harder to cut back and privatise the welfare state than the hard right in the Tory Party would have liked. Second, the Tories have considered it prudent to allow the welfare state to absorb some of the social costs of their monetarist economic policies. Therefore, rather than the wholesale 'rolling back' of the welfare state fleetingly considered in the early 1980s (the 'Think Tank' proposals of 1983 leaked to *The Economist*), Tory governments have so far conducted a war of attrition against state welfare. Divide and rule strategies have played a central part in this strategy, aided by an electoral system which has never forced the Tories to gain an absolute majority for its policies.

Both of the two major means used by the government to attack state health and welfare provision have sought to weaken the bonds of social solidarity established between and within social classes established during and after World War Two. The first method has been to attack wherever feasible the principle of universalism which was (albeit weakly) embodied in the welfare state after 1945. They have sought to magnify and exploit internal divisions among working class people, and to construct a new class alliance which convinces individuals and families that they would be better off to abandon collectivism and strike out on their own, instead of being held back by the dead weight of weaker or less enterprising members of the same class. The most dramatic success of this strategy has been in a massive retreat from public housing provision since the 1980s, spearheaded by the council house sales initiated in the early 1980s (Hills and Mullings, 1990). They have had some success in relation to social security through the provisions of the 1986 Social Security Act and other measures which sought to draw firmer distinctions between the working and nonworking poor and encouragement to private provision in pensions. The cumulative effect of these and other measures have now been shown to have resulted in a real deterioration of incomes and lifestyle for those in the 'bottom third' of society, rather than the promised 'trickle-down' of society's riches. However the expected improvements in the position of the next third have either not occurred or have been all but wiped out by the collapse of the 'British economic miracle' in the 1990s (Commission on Social Justice, 1993).

If the first method has involved individualism outside the state, the second involves the promotion of individualism within it. The new individualism has affected public service trade unions internally by challenging traditional forms of worker collectivism, for example, through the introduction of secret ballots on union executive and leadership elections or such measures as the introduction of performance related pay. The most important impact however has been upon the public services themselves where the divisions between workers as providers and as users which became apparent during the Winter of Discontent, has been elaborated into a critique and reorganisation of public provision under the doctrines of the 'new public management' (for the essential features of which, see Hunter, 1993). Where the need for public provision could not itself be challenged, the strategy has been to attack the ability of the publicly managed sector to directly provide services of quality which are responsive to the needs of individuals.

The attack began at the fringes in the early 1980s, through privatisation of hospital ancillary services and the introduction of general management into the NHS. We are now, with the consolidation of the 1990 NHS and Community Care Act in the wake of the Tories' 1992 election victory, a long way down the road towards the government's ultimate ideal, which is the complete contracting out of any publicly provided services which can not be otherwise privatised. In this respect, as with its other programmes of privatisation, the Major government has been pursuing the end-game strategy every bit as ruthlessly as any of its predecessors. A central aim of this strategy is to break any bonds of social solidarity which might exist between managers and workers in public services, and between providers and users. The government very early on abrogated the traditional role of the state to behave as a 'model' employer setting an example in pay, conditions and industrial relations (Mailly, Dimmock and Sethi, 1989). This had been based on a 'quasi-socialist' conception that public services were a superior breed of enterprise, with a social orientation to both workers and users which needed to be emulated by private industry. In trade union terms it was such notions that gave rise to Whitleyism in the public sector.

The new ideal is a further stage on: no employment responsibilities at all, through the creation of an 'enabling' state which disburses public funds with no or minimal employment responsibilities, simply monitoring and regulating standards of service to ensure that contract requirements are met. The new public management therefore announces to the world that workers' pay and conditions are not issues of public concern. In the emerging alliance between the new public managers and the consumers the service offered under the contract is all that matters, backed up in some instances (but not community care) by the Citizen's Charter. In this sense the internal separation of contracting and providing is an attempt to drive a wedge between workers and managers of services and place the latter in a pact with consumers supervised by central government, whether provision is inside or outside the state.

In the past it was presumed, particularly in health and welfare services, that outcomes were too complex to measure, and that relations between managers, workers and users were cemented to a considerable degree by a public spirited altruism. This required that both managers and users place considerable trust and hence functional autonomy in the hands of producers, literally in some instances putting 'your life in their hands'. The classic socialist defence of public services is that they replaced commoditised services which encouraged pecuniary motives rather than dedication to users' interests, by decommodified services which liberated an altruistic focus solely on the best interests of users. This was often reinforced by a professional form of organisation which granted those who benefited from it not only high economic rewards but also occupational self-government, a form of elite 'syndicalism' as Rudolf Klein (1983) called it.

The new public management challenges both of these conceptions and claims that a different style of management based on private sector approaches is most appropriate. It argues that unless checked, the tendency of those working for the state is to defend their jobs and expand their mandates. Unconstrained by market mechanisms they pressure governments to provide more and more, without considering whether it is beneficial or necessary, creating a dangerous ratchet effect in favour of increased public provision. The theory appeals to 'the public' for support to check this tendency, and to bring public sector workers to heel through new approaches to public enterprise which subject workers to increased monitoring of performance from above, and weaken powerful internal collectivities such as unions and professional associations through such means as individual contracts, intensified competition between public and private providers, and forcing public services workers to compete against each other for work.

The intellectual justification for this approach lies much less in a cosy 'welfare pluralism', than the crude new right pressure group theory of 'public choice' (eg Buchanan and Tullock, 1962). This suggests that state expenditure and provision have a natural tendency to grow as a result of a conspiracy by providers to build empires by convincing governments and publics that it is of benefit, when much of it is at best of dubious utility and through exercise of monopoly power it often fails to respond to users' needs. The interests of workers and providers are in direct conflict, and those of users can only be realised by competitive pressures which subordinate workers to providers through a system mediated by strong managerial power. The notion of altruistic public service thus holds no place

in this theory. Lurking behind it, and indeed all new right thinking, is a highly pessimistic assumption that human nature is inherently selfish and needs constantly to be constrained by market or other mechanisms if the social fabric is to be maintained. The Winter of Discontent provided fuel for this crude theory of the state by allowing the new right to portray public services trade unionists as heartless bullies who would stop at nothing (even refusing to bury the dead) in the ruthless pursuit of their selfish aims. It is also based on 'zero sum' notion of power, in which power is exercised by providers at the expense of users, unless the reverse is made to happen. The possibility that both providers and users might be jointly empowered is not entertained.

Hence the critique, very explicit within the community care reforms, of previous 'producer led' services, and the need to replace them with 'user led' services. Sir Roy Griffiths (1992 – quoted by Hunter, 1993), one of the main proponents of the new approach, argued that by the 1980s it had been widely accepted that the cautious and rule-bound approach of the 'old administrative model of public service' had resulted in the consumer, the patient or the client being neglected and in a lack of accountability by the professionals in the service. It had all the inefficiencies which derive from monopoly provision. The pressure since then has been to bring more dynamics into organisation and structure and to bring market forces to bear, on the basis that without any competition these deficiencies would never be met.

A central argument of this book has been that though such arguments and the new approaches based on them are deeply flawed, they can not be dismissed out of hand. They point to very real deficiencies in the operation and not just the funding of state health and welfare before 1979, particularly its professionally dominant and bureaucratic features, which have also been been criticised from the left and by radical social movements. Bureaucracy has led to rule bound, inflexible services which have failed to respond adequately to people's changing needs. Professional authority has come under criticism from those who believe that it is of doubtful or even negative utility, and that occupational self-regulation has failed to effectively address deficiencies in individual or collective competence (eg Wilding, 1982).

In responding to these criticisms, it is therefore necessary to do more than merely restate the traditional case for well funded publicly provided health and welfare services, which offer well paid, stable and interesting jobs which meet the needs of both users and providers. This is not to dispute the essential truth of this case, rather to say that by itself it is not enough, because it tends towards a conservative defence of the status quo. The alternative is to accept aspects of the critique, but to dispute the diagnosis and prescribed treatment. In previous chapters we have seen how the bureaucratic and professionalised aspects of state provision were strongly influenced by the limited nature of the extension of social rights and liberties within the welfare state after 1945, and the subordination of the welfare state to wider political-economic imperatives.

Arising from this analysis, there is an alternative socialist conception of public services which differs as much from the 'old administrative model' as the 'new public management', and which has been increasingly accepted by public service trade unions since the 1980s. As well as attacking the deficiencies of private provision, and the dangers of a return to the market, this approach seeks also to democratise public services through processes of individual and collective accountability to users at all levels, through structures that operate with a fairer distribution of power and rewards to all paid workers, and which provide services which do not substitute for collective remedies to disadvantage, discrimination and oppression. It also argues that, while acknowledging that there is a case for more efficient use of resources, and the development of appropriate measures of performance, achieving quality and saving costs may often be in conflict. First, because the need do more with the same amount of money will lead to the cutting of corners; second because in the public services most cost savings seek to economise on labour, and it is a highly problematic notion that increasing workloads and depressing the wages and conditions of workers enhances quality. New trade union and socialist approaches have responded to the new public management by increasingly seeking a new compact with users on the basis that both groups have a mutual interest for well trained, properly rewarded workers with manageable workloads. In return, public service workers have increasingly accepted that there is a greater need for accountability, and that public service workers need to demonstrate their worth and efficiency rather than, as too often in the past, expecting it to be taken on trust. As well as defending a universal public right to social provision, the left and trade union movement are therefore increasingly campaigning for public rights in provision.

A major flaw with new public management approaches is thus their failure to identify the root causes of the undesirable features of state services, or to take account of the possible conflicts between cost saving and quality enhancement. As a result the new public management apparently offers a means of addressing user subordination within services, but in reality this is more likely to end up replacing professional with managerial domination of need involving means testing and rationing. Its consumerism leads it into crude conceptions of worker-provider relationships which lends itself to hierarchy because it encourages a conception of the labour process in which providers produce a product that is then used by consumers, rather than seeing care as produced across this divide. The new public management also has no strategy for tackling the social causes of disadvantage because it largely takes for granted the wider social context of inequality in which public services operate, and seeks more internally ef ficient and effective ways of allocating resources. Similarly, it has no realistic strategy for dealing with the fact that inequalities of class, gender, 'race', disability and age constrain the ability of people to act as informed and assertive 'consumers'.

One major problem for the left, however, is that it still only has a rudimentary conception of what alternative approaches might mean in practice, and not least how the new information technology might assist its emergence. Partly this is because over-bureaucratised models have dominated left approaches to state organisation whether in state socialist countries or capitalist democracies. Since the 1980s however it has been compounded by the left's exclusion from power at national level and the way that Tory governments have used all the powers at their disposal to frustrate the development of new socialist approaches within the local state. So however flawed the theory of new public management, and however strong the alternative case in principle, public service workers and their organisations have faced daunting problems in maintaining unity among themselves in the face of pressures to compete individually and collectively with each other, while at the same time seeking to construct new alliances with users in competition with the new public management.

Each of the three unions now part of UNISON have sought to respond to these pressures according to the rather different circumstances in which they have found themselves. NUPE has been particularly in the front line of the attack on public provision through contracting out of ancillary and manual workers' services in health and local government. As the union most often seen, accurately or otherwise, as taking the most militant action during the Winter of Discontent, it reviewed its approach to trade union strategy in the services affected by privatisation, and its approach to wider politics. The gradual shift away from industrial action to oppose privatisation was partly dictated by the weakened position of the trade union movement, especially after Thatcher's second election victory in 1983. However there was also a recognition that traditional strike action may not always be appropriate in the public services, and there was a shift towards an approach which sought to forge a wider alliance with users, by campaigning which utilised research conducted by the union and organisations such as the Public Services Privatisation Research Unit, which has shown how contracting out threatens not just the pay and conditions of workers, and public accountability, but at the same time standards of services for users. These have been highlighted, for example, by the threats to users' health and well being posed by contracted out hospital cleaning services and school meals. At the same time as opposing contracting out, NUPE and other public service unions saw no alternative but to enter the fray and seek to keep contracts 'in-house'. Wherever possible it sought to do this by favourable deals which sought to maintain solidarity between workers and managers, though in many instances these agreements involved a worsening of pay and conditions for low paid and disadvantaged workers.

COHSE experienced some of these same pressures, but more intensely in the area of direct provision of health and welfare. COHSE in the 1980s was caught in a pincer movement between two apparently unstoppable forces, the accelerated closure of mental illness and mental handicap hospitals and shift to community care on the one hand, and the phenomenal growth of the non-TUC Royal College of Nursing, tacitly encouraged by the government, on the other. The former coincided with the rise of an increasingly vocal user's movement which was often critical of traditional psychiatry, including the role of nurses within it. The latter was associated with a renewed and individualist emphasis on professionalism among many nurses and declining support for traditional forms of trade union action, which became vulnerable to professional discipline by the nurses' regulatory body, the United Kingdom Central Council for Nursing, Midwifery and Health Visiting (UKCC). The shift away from collective bargaining and the creation of a nurses Pay Review Body, and the shift away from workplace to college based training under Project 2000, also added to the pressure on COHSE to modify the militant and instrumental trade unionism which it had successfully espoused in the 1970s.

Of the three unions considered here, NALGO, though not able to carry on 'business as usual', perhaps did not experience the need to adapt to the pressures exerted by new public management as intensely as NUPE and COHSE. In terms of membership, finance and continuing influence, NALGO was one of the success stories of the trade union movement in the 1980s. In social services it fought off an attempt by professional associations in the mid 1970s to rival its collective bargaining role. It fought a largely successful campaign to uplift the status and position of social workers through strike action in 1978-79. Its leadership maintained an independent left stance in the 1980s and won a successful ballot among the members to establish a Political Fund. It gained from the growth of local authority professional and white collar staff during the 1980s. Only with the advent of the contracting out provisions of the community care reforms and the spread of Compulsory Competitive Tendering into the heart of local government, is the membership base it set up now significantly threatened.

Starting with a detailed examination of COHSE's experiences, we will now consider in more detail how the three unions which form UNISON have sought to deal with some of the challenges posed by the shift to community care under new public management approaches. In the next chapter I will seek to develop these emerging approaches into a more general alternative approach to community care.

## COHSE, Community Care and the Shift from State Provision: A Case Study

COHSE's conversion to the radical politics of community care did not happen overnight, and sections of the membership remained uneasy about it. Only cautious steps towards change were made by the 1983 Mallinson Report, *Future of the Psychiatric Services*. This set the scene for a continuing defence of the central role of the NHS and the medical model in community care, and opposition not just to privatisation, but also to local government and voluntary sector involvement. It was not until the publication of the Griffiths Report in 1988, and the election of Hector MacKenzie as General Secretary, that a more fundamental change of heart occurred within the union, pushed forward by the younger generation of COHSE officers. One of these, Bob Abberley won support from Conference in 1988 for sentiments such as:

> We must recognise that to have comprehensive community care provision we also need the support of a whole range of services as well as health, such as social services, housing, education, home helps, social security and many others. We must get involved in this wider debate about future provision... None of us supports the devalued life some people are forced to lead. Sleeping rough in inner cities, living in run down bed and breakfast accommodation and not forgetting those in private residential homes many of whom suffer sub-standard care. We know this is not right but we also know in our hearts that there's got to be a better way than long stay hospitals. Would you like a long stay hospital to be your home? I wouldn't. Our job is to find that better way and fight for it.

This new radicalism resulted in a much more open and less insular union. COHSE started to seek more members in the private and voluntary sectors. It affiliated to the National Council for Voluntary Organisations, and for the first time started having friendly discussions with organisations like MIND and MENCAP. One of the most important products was the Working Party Report of 1989 *Future Services for People with Learning Difficulties* which questioned the appropriateness of the medical model and by implication the centrality of the NHS and nurses in provision of care (see Chandler, 1989).

How has this been reflected in changes at lower levels of the union? In the absence of systematic evidence, what follows is a thumbnail sketch in late 1992 of how one part of COHSE has been trying to come to terms with the new politics of community care – to support the progressive elements of the Griffiths reforms while opposing their negative features, and to protect their own interests in ways that advance those of users. COHSE in South East London was covered by Richard Parker, one of the younger generation of officers who was enthusiastic about the shift to community care and distinguished between the role played by the voluntary and private sectors. The transfer to the voluntary sector often occurred as a 'scam' in the 1980s. Social security was reluctant to fund board and lodging payments to patients leaving hospital because it was claimed that the NHS had already funded their care. Consortia were then set up under which staff continued to be employed by the NHS, but ex-patients became tenants of housing associations, thus entitling them to assistance from social security.

Such deals helped to carry forward the closure programme of Darenth Park (for the wider context of which see Korman and Glennerster, 1985). Richard Parker has no doubt that this has enhanced the status and way of life of residents, but has more mixed feelings about the union implications. Not only has the quality of life of residents often improved immeasurably through some of the carefully planned and developed schemes – they have their own flats, a comfortable way of life, access to shops, training centres and social facilities – but there has been a fundamental change in their relationship with staff. Many are schemes where COHSE members continued to be employed as mental handicap nurses. However they no longer work with patients, or clients, but with tenants, who have rights to privacy and autonomy which must be respected, and which housing associations like Hexagon have been anxious to emphasise. From a union point of view the voluntary sector is an unpredictable quantity. It has grown very rapidly and often has not developed sufficient industrial relations expertise.

In this area of London COHSE sought to respond to very rapidly changing circumstances. As part of the review of expenditure and priorities within an internal market, health authorities are re-examining their arrangements with consortia, and a more wholesale transfer to the voluntary sector of staff as well as buildings is now taking place. I accompanied Richard Parker to a branch meeting at Arnold House, a Directly Managed Unit (DMU) of Greenwich Health Authority, where health staffs' and tenants' future had been put out to tender among voluntary associations, and they were awaiting the results of the auction. From an industrial relations point of view, the transfer was being handled with care by the health authority. A condition of the transfer was that on day one the successful voluntary association would have to re-employ nurses on their existing grades and terms and conditions, which would include union recognition (an approach which the European Community has endorsed through its Transfer of Undertakings (Protection of Employment Regulations) (TUPE) – see later in this chapter).The branch secretary, Bram Appaddo, who had previously been a charge nurse in Darenth Park, and the 15 or so members present, most of them women and many of them black, were naturally anxious about the future. They realised that as soon as they were re-employed there was nothing to stop their new employer from immediately giving notice that they wished to change terms and conditions of service.

Arnold House is a 'core and cluster' development of the kind that was seen as innovatory in the early 1980s, but which has rapidly become dated. Everyone agreed it was really a kind of 'mini-institution' in the community, as Bram called it. Most of the tenants are in their middle and later years, and had come from Darenth Park. There are four sets of flats and a total of 32 residents, grouped around central facilities, including the day room where the union meeting was taking place. It is an attractively-built complex, set back from a main road near shops, next to a health centre. Staff think it is too big and institutional and foresee a shift to smaller units, even buying up individual houses in the community, with 'independent living' as the way forward in the future, though some residents are said to be anxious about the prospect. The staff are hoping that a takeover by a housing association might facilitate such a shift.

The biomedical model is still influential in that every resident is attached to a consultant psychiatrist. There are reserve powers under the Mental Health Act to compel co-operation from residents. Though I got the impression that there is considerable respect for residents' autonomy, I was not able to talk to any residents. There are standing arrangements for advocacy with the local MENCAP. Staff, although anxious about the future, were not defensive. As Bram put it to me:

> Staff know there has to be change, and are prepared for it as long as terms and conditions are protected. As long as they've got security. Everybody's got mortgages, family and so on.

Prospects look relatively optimistic here, though this was perhaps not typical of developments in this area of South London. It was proving much more difficult to recruit and protect the terms and conditions of workers in the rapidly growing private sector. NALGO however had a significant amount of membership in housing associations and the voluntary sector. The new contracting environment, and the crisis in local authority finance is likely, Richard Parker believed, to drive standards, including wages and conditions, downwards. Already the shortfall between social security contributions to residential care and the full cost of providing a service was affecting standards and driving many homes out of business even before social security money is transferred to local authorities. A major difficulty was the inadequacy of the arrangements for inspection, which will not be sufficiently strengthened by the 1990 Act. Visits were too infrequent to make a difference, and he was concerned that local authority Inspection Units would not be truly independent and that the need to contract out would encourage a relaxation of standards. However he has had some success in improving conditions by union support of 'whistle-blowers', who expose poor standards of care. Nursing homes will continue to be monitored and regulated by health authorities and research has shown that most opt to take a minimal and often ineffective policing role rather than developing a more interventionist emphasis on ensuring 'quality' (Arai, 1993). There is no reason to expect that local authority regulation of residential homes will in general be any different.

My informal discussions with union officials from other parts of the country confirm this picture of the difficulties in recruiting and organising workers in the residential and nursing home sectors. On the whole the union appears primarily to offer individual support for members in cases of disciplinary action – what one officer called 'a Citizen's Advice Bureau role', – or through indemnity insurance. The latter is often used as a means of convincing home owners that union membership is also in their interests too. Because of the fragmented nature of ownership and the relatively small size of workplaces, it is proving difficult to establish collective organisation of a stable kind which could secure formal recognition, facilities and begin bargaining with employers. There is widespread agreement that much more union effort needs to be put into this sector, particularly since it is growing so fast, and that the resources available to UNISON might make this a much more viable proposition. As Jean Geldert (1993), then Chairperson of NALGO's Local Government Committee, pointed out, though there is no legal requirement to separate out the purchasing and providing functions in community care, many local authorities have moved enthusiastically down this road, 'applying the Compulsory Competitive Tendering (CCT) ethos and even the CCT rules to community care'. This separation of functions facilitates privatisation and a deterioration in working conditions. Social services departments may have been hierarchical but still had a 'professional' ethos, but the spread of contract culture formalises relationships and creates a rigid separation between those who decide, and those who provide. As Geldert suggests, this creates an environment where quality considerations take second place to saving costs, which in a labour intensive service necessarily involve, alongside rationing and means-testing, a deterioration of working conditions, not just by privatisation but also in the public sector:

> The result is lower pay, shorter hours for part time staff, the squeezing of unsocial hours payments and lower staffing levels overall. Fewer skilled staff are being employed and there will be a higher turnover. Many authorities have already cut home care hours so that only quasi nursing support is available but not the housework or therapy essential to quality of life (Geldert, 1993).

## Conditions of Work in Community Care

What is required is an audit of the employment effects of community care as a whole across health and social care, and as it will affect particular sectors in public, commercial and voluntary care. A good starting point is

NALGO's briefing paper on the Act sent out to branches (NALGO, 1990a). This points out that the reforms will put enormous pressure on staff in the community whether they work in the public or the independent sectors. In the local authority sector scarce resources will be diverted into the bureaucracy necessary for inspection, assessment and contracting, and established relationships will be subject to rapid and uncertain change.

The picture that emerges from COHSE's responses in the 1980s is of a union that was prepared to go beyond a defence of the status quo, and even to recognise that government reforms had progressive aspects. For example COHSE's commentary on the 1990 Bill as it passed through Parliament, *Community Care: Which Way Forward?* welcomed the central position accorded to local government in community care, the emphasis on needs assessment, the recognition – up to a point – of the needs of black and ethnic minority people, and above all the requirement to plan care and involve users and local people in its provision:

> COHSE wishes to see a community care system which is fair, universal and under democratic control, which empowers the service users, values service workers and actively involves them in promoting high standards, and which genuinely meets the needs of people.

At a more local level COHSE in the South West set up a Care in the Community Forum, which was active in producing a number of policy documents, ranging from responses to the 1989 White Paper, *Caring for People*, to more focused topics such as 'challenging behaviour' among people with learning difficulties. The discussion document *Community Care: Current Issues* argues that good community care will require workers receiving management support for the greater 'risk' taking in providing liberties for users.

The Forum is an example of how trade unionists at a local level have been seeking to confront community care issues in a positive way. Another is the way in which in 1992 COHSE/NALGO/NUPE in the West Midlands, anticipating the formation of UNISON, jointly produced *Quality Care – It's Only Fair* which states a strong commitment for well-resourced and democratically organised community care, accountable to all workers and users.

In the independent sector, contracting threatens to worsen conditions, create insecurity and lower pay. There is a close connection between these deteriorating conditions for users, and their likely health and safety effects on staff. COHSE began to develop special briefings for community staff on health and safety prior to its merger with NALGO and NUPE. These pointed out that employers still have a responsibility for health and safety under law, even when the workplace is someone's home. Such a responsibility is harder to enforce in the independent sector, by virtue of its

## Occupational stress in the public services

A report by the Health Education Authority (HEA, 1987) examined occupational stress in a range of public service occupations and concluded that this was due to the properties of 'service' jobs themselves and the way they were organised and managed, and not just the result of attitudes which workers brought to their jobs

### Sources of Stress
NURSES
*Clients and Their Problems* Dealing with anxiety, sickness, pain and death; supporting others with little training on how to support oneself
*Public Expectations* Expected to control feelings without outward shows of emotion
*Role Conflict* Trying to balance the conflicting expectations of different groups, including fellow nurses, relatives, other professionals and management; demands of the job and circumstances, such as shift work, disruptive to outside life and relationships
*Reorganisation and Change* Rapid managerial change in context where resources are stretched
*Resources* Inadequate resources to fulfill responsibilities; stress caused by low pay and poor conditions

SOCIAL WORKERS
*Clients and Their Problems* Increase in severity of problems which cannot easily be solved, eg due to poverty, unemployment and poor housing
*Public Expectations* Public mistrust or hostility to social workers - 'damned if they do and damned if they don't'
*Role Conflict* Difficulties in deciding whom to help, and when to invoke legal powers
*Reorganisation and Change* Generic role, increased legal responsibilities and authoritarian management
*Resources* Overwhelmed by clients' demands due to severity and extent of social problems

### Effects of Stress
These are defined as behavioural, physical and emotional, with both short and long term effects. They affect personal relationships.

NURSES Higher than average rates of smoking and alcohol abuse, back injury, absenteeism and 'wastage', and suicide

SOCIAL WORKERS Violent attacks by clients; pronounced tendency to disillusion and even 'burn-out' fragmented nature, and because employers are often hostile to unions. One of the most important health and safety issues in care is, of course, lifting. Back injury is a major health hazard in social care and it is likely to increase as workloads increase, and in the absence of proper lifting equipment in people's homes or in the private sector. Community care has its own particular hazards of harassment or assault associated with working alone without the ability to call on colleagues for support (Rogers and Salvage, 1987).

Stress is very much a health hazard in community care as in other forms of public service work (Health Education Authority, 1987). To the extent to which it leads to improved relations with users and more satisfying, less custodial work, community care can potentially reduce stress. However, the circumstances in which community care is being implemented, through imposed change involving less secure pay and conditions, with inadequate resources, are likely to increase occupational stress in two ways. First, workers will continue to get caught in the 'service trap' (Dressel, 1982) and try personally to bridge the widening care gap, at a cost to their own health. Second, if my arguments in the previous chapter are correct, staff will inevitably be implicated in more explicit rationing of services, they will become professionally frustrated and seen increasingly as the 'street level bureaucrats' who have to impose such decisions on users (Lipsy, 1980). Very little research has been done in this area, but it is not surprising that available findings, such as the study by Jocelyn Handy (1991) of occupational stress among psychiatric nurses, found similar stress levels whether nurses worked in hospital or the community.

All these developments add up to increased levels of occupational stress for employed workers as they compete against each other for work, or are shunted from one sector to another with little consultation, against a background of increasing needs and inadequate resources. The changes also promise to increase conflict with users and carers, as the increased expectations raised by the reforms lead to disappointment and even anger at the rationing decisions which community care staff will be forced to implement. On the positive side there is increasing recognition that stress is a trade union health and safety issue which is every bit as important as more tangible physical hazards, which can contribute significantly to risk of injury and to work related mental and physical ill-health. Particularly in the human services there are contradictions in services which claim to have a 'caring' face and yet subject paid workers to such high levels of stress. In recent years COHSE, NALGO and NUPE have raised their campaigning profile around such issues, and constructed a broader bargaining agenda. This has included publication of negotiating guides on such issues as childcare, sexual and racial harassment, parental and special leave, and rights of part-timers and workers with disabilities. In 1992 COHSE produced a set of *Guidelines on Tackling Stress from Health Care*

*Work,* which in the context of UNISON need to be broadened to all forms of caring and public service work.

## Continuing Divisions between Health and Social Care

An assumed distinction between health care and social care is a constant theme throughout the community care reforms but it is nowhere precisely defined. The partial exception to this is mental health where, partly due to pressure from the Royal College of Psychiatrists, and other interest groups, the NHS is to retain a central role. COHSE, though welcoming the provision of ring-fenced funds (the specific grant), criticised this because of a concern that it would lead to too much emphasis on the medical as opposed to the social needs of users of mental health services. The old mental hospitals may be closing, but the battle continues about what will replace them. A choice broadly exists between two main alternatives which involve a limited or more whole-hearted shift to a progressive community care policy. On the one hand, there is a medicalised approach with District General hospital beds as the linchpin of provision, and with reinforced powers for psychiatrists (the proposed 'Supervised Discharge Orders') to remove patients from community 'parole' if they fail to follow prescribed drug treatments, or make nuisances of themselves, or are a risk to self or others (Royal College of Psychiatrists, 1993). Alternatively, there is a more social and pluralistic approach based on the availability to users of a range of medical and non medical alternative services in the locality, within an anti-discriminatory framework of improved rights and protected liberties (Rogers, Pilgrim and Lacey, 1992; MIND, 1992b. While debate continues as to the extent to which contracting facilitates provision of a broader range of alternatives, the proposed powers of supervised discharge will consolidate the traditional 'drugs plus spells in hospitals approach' to mental distress in the new age of community care.

In practice the distinction between health and social needs is an artificial one, and is already leading to nonsensical practices in domiciliary care in which bathing is defined as health and washing as social care (Brindle, 1991; National Association of Health Authorities and Trusts, 1992). Considerable confusion remains as to how to provide a 'seamless service' between so many public, private and voluntary sector occupations and agencies (George, 1992). The giving of medication is another area of dispute between health and social services. As Richard Parker pointed out to me, it costs much more for a nurse to administer it than a home help or regraded care assistant. There is a case for enlarging home help responsibilities. Such decisions however should be made on policy and professional rather than simply economic grounds. In practice, as we saw above, this is happening in the context of increased rationing of access to such services. Assistance with housework is being withdrawn, and workers are being transferred to caring duties as cheap substitutes for nurses. The Preliminary Report of NUPE's Home Carers Survey in 1990 estimated that 17 per cent of local authority or independent sector home helps and care assistants carry out 'nursing tasks' such as administering drugs, changing catheters and dressings, testing urine, injections, and assisting in stoma care. Yet only just over half have received training, very rarely in areas relevant to nursing care (NUPE, 1990b). As Parsley Power-Smith and Mary Evans (1992) argue, in the context of caring for older people with dementia, this often involves unjustifiable exploitation of home care workers. Sociological studies of home care workers show that they are readily exploitable as a result of their high degree of commitment to users (Warren, 1990). The Final Report of the NUPE Survey is discussed later in this chapter

Under pressure from the internal market, health authorities throughout Britain are undertaking ruthless 'skill mix' reviews among community nurses and health visitors, the aim of which is often, not as might be imagined, to determine objectively the levels of trained staff needed, but as far as possible to reduce and substitute them. In parts of the Trent region over 60 per cent of G and H (highest grade) district nurses and health visitors are to be replaced by D and even lower grades. Current postholders are to be made redundant, take unpaid 'career breaks' or placed in lower graded posts (COHSE, 1992a). As NUPE Guidelines (1993) point out, despite firm research evidence such as that by Carr-Hill et al (1993) that higher grade nursing staff provide a better quality of care, cost pressures are leading to increasing substitution by cheaper and less well trained staff. Radical proposals like those of Roger Dyson, an industrial relations adviser to the Department of Health, outlined in *Changing Labour Utilisation in NHS Trusts*, not only ignore such evidence but seek to take the process much further and employ a small 'core' of staff and a casualised mass of contracted workers with few if any rights (Wing, 1992).

This is just part of a more general trend in which community nursing staff are taking on extra responsibilities as a result of earlier discharge of high dependency patients through 'quicker and sicker' regimes. These patients are as we have seen now increasingly being off-loaded on to local authority staff who have often not been properly trained to undertake them. At the same time as demands for care increase, partly because of growing numbers of frail older people, and partly because NHS hospitals are off-loading care, numbers of district nurses stagnate and the number of health visitors in training is falling (George, 1992). It is likely in future that higher grade nurses in the community will be found less frequently in care and more often as health authority 'care managers' assessing needs and devising 'packages of care' to be delivered by others (Mason, 1992).

Around nine per cent of NHS expenditure in 1988-89 for England and Wales was spent on community services, and more than half of this went on community nursing, midwifery and health visiting. Skill mix exercises will enable these costs to be contained at the same time as activity is increased. As Christina Potrykus (1992) points out:

> The Audit Commission has calculated that £30 million a year could be saved by replacing grade G or above district nurses with half-cost health care assistants.

Not only does this suggest that we may be witnessing the early stages of a massive deskilling of community nursing, but the relationships of nurses to their work may also be undergoing significant change. According to Potrykus, the growing importance of medically-dominated Family Health Service Authorities (FHSA) in community care, and the growth of GP fundholders, is leading to a growing subordination of community nurses within practices, shifting them away from the ideals of independent patch-based practice advocated by the Cumberlege Report. Preventive work is most at risk as increasing care needs take priority. School nurses are being cut in many areas. Health Visitors are also under threat from United Kingdom Central Council for Nursing Midwifery and Health Visiting proposals in the wake of Project 2000 to create a multi-skilled 'community health care nurse' carrying out preventive and caring responsibilities.

General practitioners themselves, though they will be important players in the new community care, are generally unprepared for their role. A survey by the British Medical Association undertaken a few months prior to the April 1993 implementation date showed that at least four out of five general practitioners were unaware of the collaborative arrangements between health and social service professionals (Thomas, 1993). How GPs will fit into the system in practice remains unclear. On the one hand they will be tempted to leave care management up to social service departments, especially since they feel already overburdened and remuneration arrangements for their participation have not so far been agreed. On the other hand, many will wake up to the fact that they can no longer recommend someone for residential care and get the Department of Social Security to pick up the bill. As a result, they may enter the fray as patient advocates against local authority social workers who will be under greater pressures to ration access to care from their superiors (Leedham and Wistow, 1993). Either way, particularly in the context of the interprofessional rivalries identified by Dalley (1989), there is considerable scope for misunderstanding and conflict.

The residential care sector is similarly divided into nursing home (health) and residential (social) care, with different registration and inspection arrangements, which will continue to be divided between health authority and social services departments. The shift to a social from a health model of care could in the right context be seen as a progressive move. In the context of the community care reforms, however, much of the pressure to shift from health to social care definitions will be financially driven by the pressure on the NHS to withdraw from long term care.

This is best offset by attempts to make sure that social care is not the cheap option. In the local government sector itself, attempts are being made to improve residential care, albeit severely constrained by the financial circumstances of local authorities. This has been partly in response to the recognition, as the Wagner Report (1988) on residential care put it that residential services were in a 'demoralised state'. As well as addressing this by enhancing the rights of residents through standard-setting based on such policy documents as *Home Life: a Code of Practice for Residential Care*, produced in 1984 by the Centre for Policy on Ageing, there is at least formal recognition that training of staff is needed. What Griffiths and *Caring For People*, perhaps surprisingly, make no mention of is the need to improve wages and conditions to make social care an attractive arena to work in. Yet as COHSE's evidence to the Howe Committee set up jointly by the NJIC for Local Authorities and the Local Management Board puts it:

> For too long a majority of Britain's 300,000 residential care staff have been exploited... Pay and conditions have been neglected to a point whereby residential care no longer attracts or retains high calibre, good quality staff of all grades (COHSE, 1991, paragraph 6.1).

The evidence pointed out how few trained staff worked in this sector, and the 1991 pay award meant that many staff earned less than £100 for a 39-hour week, way below the Council of Europe Decency Threshold. It argued that while standard-setting, emphasis on rights, and training were necessary, it was necessary to move to a situation where staff are regarded as a valuable resource.

This heightened concern of COHSE with pay and conditions in the residential care sector was partly influenced by a need to raise its profile in an area where it now wished to recruit members to replace those lost as the NHS continued to withdraw from provision of long term care. In the process its distinctive approach sometimes differed from that adopted by NUPE and NALGO, the more established unions within this sector. All three unions have increasingly emphasised the importance of quality in opposition to the government's over-riding concern to contain costs. As part of this NUPE and COHSE have put considerable emphasis on training, particularly the new National Vocational Qualifications (NVQs) which have emerged in the 1980s. They have done this to counter the deskilling tendencies inherent in the new public management, in the hope also that it will lead to enhanced pay and conditions and job satisfaction, and at the same time improve the quality of service provided to users. Beyond this COHSE, partly in order to compete more effectively with the Royal College of Nursing (RCN) embraced professionalism to a greater degree than NALGO and NUPE. It saw in the UKCC's Code of Professional Ethics an opportunity to combat cost-cutting and defend of standards of care, despite the fact that discipline and deregistration by the UKCC can lead to loss of employment for a qualified nurse.

In response to continuing crises and highly publicised scandals since the 1980s, which have affected both field social work (eg Cleveland) and residential care ('pin down' in Staffordshire, Frank Beck in Leicestershire), the response of the social work establishment has been to seek to emulate the kind of approach adopted by nurses through the UKCC. This would involve a quid pro quo with the government, involving the creation of statutory body under which social work would agree to patrol standards and discipline wrongdoers, while at the same time getting government approval for a fully fledged professional register. This in essence are the proposals contained in *Safeguarding Standards*, the Report in 1991 of Roy Parker, Professor of Social Administration at Bristol University, which recommended the setting up of a General Social Services Council (GSSC) to register and exercise professional discipline over social workers.

Both the details and fundamental aspects of these proposals have generated considerable controversy. COHSE, operating in an environment where both professional and managerial discipline was not unusual, initially embraced the proposals with enthusiasm, but subsequently argued for a separate council to cover social care in both the statutory and independent sectors. NALGO, though not opposing a national body to supervise standards, expressed its opposition to the professional register proposed by Roy Parker, for a variety of reasons, including its objection to the 'double jeopardy' involved in social workers being subject to both managerial and professional discipline. The existing body, the Central Council for Education and Training in Social Work (CCETSW) set up in 1970, has not exercised such powers. NUPE on the whole kept on 'open mind' on the issues involved.

The differences between COHSE and NALGO and the uncertainty shown by NUPE illustrate how, though each union has responded positively in the 1980s to the new emphasis on such quality issues as standards, training, and accountability of workers who deal with potentially vulnerable people, the way they have tackled these can vary according to the experiences and philosophies of the trade unions involved. There are thus no ready made solutions to the organising dilemmas of public service unions in the 1990s. As it happens, the future of the Parker proposals looks uncertain at the time of writing. The government, in the shape of the junior health Minister, Tim Yeo, has expressed doubts about the feasibility of a statutory GSSC that according to some estimates might need to register up to one million workers. He has instead expressed his preference for a non-statutory 'code of practice' for social workers, particularly those working in child care. This would not subject workers to double jeopardy, but whether it would do much to protect or promote standards of care is another matter (Brindle, 1993).

Radical reform of residential care is urgently necessary, and it is significant that the fundamental problems of this sector have received little attention in official documents like the Griffiths Report in the run up to the 1990 reforms. The proposals which came out of the Howe Report (Local Government Board, 1992) were also timid and minor in scope. Trade union strategies to uplift the standing and position of residential care work, overwhelmingly staffed by low paid women workers, have only proved partially successful. Attempts by NALGO in 1983-84 to repeat their success of 1978-79 with field workers, and uplift the pay and status of residential care workers in the 'professional' sector through a campaign of industrial action, had not proved successful, by the union's own admission (NALGO, 1985). However, tentative steps on the road to improvement have included, in the manual sector, the 1987 local government job evaluation scheme which, admittedly within a pay structure characterised by low pay, uprated the position of (largely female) care assistants, by recognising the importance of 'caring skills'. The other glimmer of hope for the future is the development of the NVQ system of training initiated through the Care Sector Consortium which from 1992 became 'integrated', that is qualifications are recognised across the whole care sector – local government, NHS, commercial and voluntary sectors. In principle these will facilitate the reskilling of social care. In practice, they may encourage a 're-profiling' involving substitution of cheaper NVQ-trained for more fully trained staff. NVQ training is mainly restricted to work with older people, and it is by no means certain to what extent the commercial and voluntary sectors will take on training responsibilities.

Nevertheless public services unions have embraced training both out of a commitment to quality, and because they have seen it as a means of upskilling and uplifting low paid care workers.

Meanwhile, the numbers of scandals in residential care continue to mount, and contracting and cost pressures restrict improvement in pay and conditions, encouraging a 'cost effective' shift to the independent sector. Inevitably, in a labour intensive service, savings can only be made at the expense of staff pay and conditions. Defining work as requiring fewer rather than more skilled workers, and as requiring social rather than health care will intensify the competition and conflict between occupations and sectors. The field is thus ripe for continuing and perhaps even intensified 'border disputes' shaped by cost pressures and professional interests of the kind which previously hampered the development of effective community care (Hudson, 1992; Wistow, 1990).

## Europe to the Rescue?

The Tory government may well have ratified the Maastricht Treaty without the Social Chapter (although that may not be the end of the story), but it cannot evade all its statutory obligations to workers which flow from its membership of the European Community. One of the most significant of these, which strengthens workers' ability to oppose privatisation which leads to worse pay, conditions and union rights is under TUPE – the Transfer of Undertakings (Protection of Employment) Regulations issued by the government in 1981. These had come about as a result of the Acquired Rights Directive of 1977 under which workers' rights, including union recognition, are protected when 'an undertaking, business or part of a business' is transferred from one employer to another. When this was made part of British law under TUPE in 1981 the Tory government excluded employment which was 'not in the nature of a commercial undertaking', thus giving the green light to a decade of privatisation, contracting out and compulsory competitive tendering (CCT), all of which were expressly designed to lower costs by worsening pay and conditions, and weakening union rights.

This has now been found to be unlawful by the European Court of Justice in a judgement with clear implications for community care. In the Netherlands Mr Bartol, an employee of the Dr Sophie Redmond Stichting brought a case under the Directive and won, when the voluntary sector drugs counselling service he worked for was closed down after the local authority switched their grant support to another organisation. In Britain the key test case has been the case for unfair dismissal brought by a group of Eastbourne dustmen who were sacked in 1990 after a CCT exercise awarded the contract to the French owned company Onyx (K Milne, 1993). The Employment Appeals Tribunal has decided that the award of the refuse collection contract to Onyx was a transfer covered by the Regulations, and the way is potentially open for thousands of compensation cases (S Milne, 1993). It will also have a significant effect on contracting in the future. Councils and health authorities will have to make TUPE a condition of tendering, or risk liability for future compensation claims (COHSE/NALGO/NUPE in UNISON, 1993). UNISON is currently running a series of test cases which help establish the application of the Regulations for community care transfers. Though TUPE will not halt contracting out altogether, it does give workers and unions a powerful lever and a more promising basis from which to make in house bids. It will also better ensure that quality standards are maintained in privatised services. UNISON and other public service unions can now run campaigns among privatised workers by offering the prospect of compensation claims against authorities.

The other promising European avenue of union action is in health and safety. At a time when the Tories are continuing their attack on trade union rights through the 1993 Trade Union Reform Act, the Management of Health and Safety at Work Regulations, which came into effect on 1 January 1993 actually extend union rights in health and safety. They implement the European Community's 'Framework Directive' adopted in 1989 'to encourage improvements in the safety and health of workers at work' throughout the community (Allen and Mather, 1992).

The Regulations incorporate the 1974 Health and Safety at Work Act and place new duties on employers who employ more than five employees to ensure safe workplaces, which includes undertaking and acting upon thorough 'risk assessments' of workplace hazards. The Regulations assert the principle that the main responsibility for ensuring health and safety lies with the employers, who are required to ensure that workplaces are made safe for all those who might reasonably use them, including people with disabilities. Union safety representatives have rights to be consulted on any measures which might affect their members before changes are made to workplaces, including rights of access to appropriate information. Perhaps most important of all, whereas previously employers only needed to provide facilities to carry out workplace inspections, they must now provide safety representatives with facilities and assistance necessary to carry out all their functions. This could include time off, office space, photocopying etc. Alongside these Regulations other more specific European health and safety directives came into force in 1993, including those relating to workplace standards, work equipment, protective clothing, manual handling and new technology (COHSE, 1992; NUPE, 1992).

The Regulations and the new powers for safety representatives will also aid in the campaign against cost cutting community care which increases health and safety risks to workers and employees alike. Campaigning around health and safety standards in community care, whether in the statutory, commercial or voluntary sector, is therefore a potential means of recruiting members, and forging alliances with user groups.

## The Battle of Ideas – Examples from COHSE, NALGO and NUPE

In the struggle to deal with the effects of new public management policies in the 1980s union research has proved a vital tool in exposing the effects of government policies, developing defensive strategies, and in articulating and campaigning for alternative policies which are 'user centred and worker friendly'. In the process industrial relations and social policy issues have become inextricably enmeshed as unions like COHSE, NALGO and NUPE have sought common cause with users and pressure groups in the campaign for well-funded, publicly run, quality public services, which are responsive to the needs and wishes of users. This book has already leant heavily on the research conducted or sponsored during the 1980s and this chapter appropriately concludes with summary discussions of recent innovative research published by each of the three unions on the eve of their absorption into UNISON. The first example is NUPE's research into the changing role of home carers, then NALGO's research on users' experiences of community care, and finally COHSE's Guidelines on empowering users of mental health services.

In recent years NUPE has been giving a high profile to community care issues. In its campaign against what was then the 1990 NHS and Community Care Bill it drew attention to the fact that:

> The government's so called NHS reforms have over shadowed their proposals for community care. But care in the community is just as important. It affects almost everyone. It is particularly important to women, who are the majority of paid and unpaid carers (NUPE, 1990c).

It exposed the hidden agenda behind the transfer of community care to local authorities, of shortfalls in resourcing, cuts and privatisation, lowering of standards, and greater impositions upon unpaid carers. It called for a 'caring alternative' involving increased funding, more support for informal carers, tight controls on private residential care, a massive investment in training of health and social service employees, and user and staff involvement in community care planning.

*Bringing it All Home: the NUPE Home Care Survey* (NUPE/UNISON 1993), charts the impact of the current community care reforms on the home help/carer, profiles their pay and conditions, and maps a way forward for the future, which would enhance their role in community care services, in ways consistent with user centred and worker friendly principles. It starts by outlining the rapid changes which are taking place in the home help service, involving a shift from their traditional role as domestic helps to their increasing involvement in providing social care. The Report acknowledges that the previous provision of domestic help was unsatisfactory.

Many old people – eighty per cent – received no help at all and those who did were often old people living alone, with preferential service often given to older men. Carers received little domestic help. There is little evidence that the amount of domestic help given varied according to need, giving rise to doubts that it played a proper role in maintaining older people in their homes and preventing admission to residential care.

Although it is difficult to generalise given the widely differing practices of local authorities, the community care reforms, in the context of growing numbers of older people, the withdrawal of the NHS from long term care, and severe resource constraints on local authorities, are all leading to a rapid and widespread restructuring of the service. This is involving increased rationing and 'targeting' of services on vulnerable older people. Local authorities – as we saw earlier – are increasingly restricting provision of domestic help, privatising it or levying hefty charges. At the same time there is a pronounced shift occurring away from the provision of domestic help to the provision of personal care for frail and vulnerable older people, including washing and bathing, administration of drugs, care of catheters and appliances, and the changing of dressings. Although the current market for domiciliary care is relatively small, with five hundred agencies providing for an estimated 45,000 vulnerable older people, this can be expected to grow considerably in future as local authorities are forced to spend the bulk of the transferred social security money in the independent sector. The more rapid the shift of services from private residential to domiciliary care, the more rapidly this market will emerge, and lead to the entry of larger more profit hungry enterprises. Unlike residential care and nursing homes, there are no legal requirements however inadequate for registration and inspection in domiciliary care, as the NUPE Report points out.

The impact of this restructuring on home helps/carers themselves varies. Where they remain primarily domestic carers they may have hours cut or be transferred to the private sector. Or alternatively they may have increased caring responsibilities loaded on to them, with very little training or enhanced pay. In most authorities, caring and domestic help is being separated, while in some a group of generic carers is being created who may work in both residential and domiciliary care. As the Report puts it, home helps/carers 'are caught in the middle of the confusion surrounding "health care" and "social care" that is making joint planning between health and local authorities a nightmare' (p. 11).

NUPE's survey of 1200 home helps/carers in the UK profiles some of these effects. It discovered that most respondents were white middle aged women with considerable experience and domestic responsibilities of their own. The majority were extremely low paid and many worked unpaid overtime. Two thirds were not in their employers' sick pay or pension schemes because of their part-time or casual status. There had been a sig-

## Some views of home carers as expressed in the NUPE Home Care survey

The times (for clients) have been cut so much, we haven't hardly time to say 'Hello' never mind listening to their problems.

Most home helps do lots of extra work involving shopping (when we do our own) plus lots of other favours we don't like to say no to.

We are constantly being told we must cut time down as we have a budget of hours to work within.

Lifting aids and even essential handrails are taking months rather than weeks to be installed.

I have not yet had even one hour's training!

More training should be given in lifting and catheters. I am now doing home care with no training at all and I have had to ask the client if they can show me how to do the emptying of catheter bags, etc... I have also found it hard in the beginning when home care first came in to actually wash clients, especially men, with no training.

Most home helps feel very fed up with the present changes. We are being strictly kept to our contracted hours or under, yet we are asked to pull in extra hours... So instead of having five clients in one day we get seven clients but no more pay... We are being asked to look after patients with mental health problems, child abuse victims, and families with problems and this causes a lot of home helps a lot of stress and anxiety.

I am worried that my work is not eligible for pension rights.

On the matter of holiday pay, at the moment we do not get any.

If this job is done properly... then it is a job which holds a great deal of responsibility and skill, and I feel there is a real need for upgrading, both in salary and position.

nificant shift towards involvement of personal care against a background of generally increased workloads. For example one third administered medicines and were involved in other 'nursing' activities, for which many of them had not received training. A quarter of respondents were unaware of health and safety procedures. A significant number expressed reservations about becoming involved in personal care, some because they were embarrassed about washing and bathing clients, particularly if they were men. The NUPE Report points to other research evidence which indicates that users are also often unhappy about receiving personal care from home helps.

In charting these developments the NUPE Report is only too aware that in the short run local authorities' room for manoeuvre is severely restricted by legislation and their own parlous financial position. It provides detailed advice to union negotiators on how to deal with these changes. At present most home helps are graded within the 1987 Job Evaluation scheme of the National Joint Council as manual workers. NUPE argues that increased responsibilities should either by rewarded by upgrading within the scheme or regrading within the Administrative, Professional and Technical Services Council (APTC) at a level sufficiently high to compensate for loss of overtime and other enhanced payments. It calls for full rights for part-time workers, including an end to their casual status and inclusion in pension schemes, holiday pay and other rights available to full time workers. Drug administration and other responsibilities should only be taken on with the express consent of community nurses. It calls for protection of transferred workers' rights under the TUPE provisions. In the longer run, the Report does not oppose change, but argues that if the home help/care service is to be transformed and improved this will require substantial investment (p. 16).

This sets an ambitious agenda of reform for UNISON, including the full integration of the service into health and social services, the continuing provision of free domestic care to older people, greater assistance within services to carers, training for home helps/carers under National Vocation Qualifications (NVQs), and rights to participation in the planning of community care services.

The second example of recent union research on community care is NALGO's Report, written up by Lindsay Mackie, *Community Care: Users' Experiences* (Mackie, 1992). In contrast to the large scale survey undertaken by NUPE, this is intensive qualitative rather than quantitative research into the experiences of sixteen users of community care, with a range of disabilities. The research, undertaken for NALGO by the Institute for Public Policy Research, involved interviews with users, informal and formal carers, and some managers. All people bar one were living in their own homes and many in a previous era would most likely have been confined in institutions. Indeed some respondents had previously experienced institutional care, and were generally in no doubt about which they preferred:

Our most striking impression from conducting these interviews was that the idea of community care was a wonderful one and hence must be made to work. No matter how hard it is for a person with severe disabilities, with profound learning difficulties, with recurrent mental illness, to live in the community, it was what they overwhelmingly want (p 4).

The aim of the research was to shift discussion of community care away from generalised issues of policy, and to ground it in a better understanding of what is happening at the level of service provision, taking account of paid workers' and managers' view, but giving a primacy to the views and wishes of users themselves. Although, as we have already seen, the NALGO Report openly sides with the shift to community care, it expresses some doubts about what it will mean in practice. The transfer of social security money to local authorities will involve a shift to a more discretionary system based on needs assessment, in a context of limited resources, and the absence of comprehensive anti-discriminatory legislation for people with disabilities. It points out that the Disabled Persons (Services, Consultation and Representation) Act 1986, which requires that disabled people and their organisations be involved in planning of provision has never been fully implemented by either central or local government. More recently a private members' Bill to outlaw discrimination against people with disabilities, introduced during the Parliamentary session leading up to the April 1993 implementation date for community care, was not supported by the government and subsequently fell.

In practice then, good intentions on community care may be tempered by harsh economic realities and also bad practices by agencies and professionals involved. The Report highlights the dilemmas of local authorities as they struggle to cope with such pressures. The interviews with paid workers showed that they often felt in a dilemma about whether to seek out unmet need, only to be confronted with an inability to meet it. Some respondents said that the 1989 Children's Act was being prioritised by social services departments over community care provision. The impression gained was that even where local authorities were willing, the lack of resources was leading away from provision to management of scarcity; crisis management instead of prevention; and waiting lists meant that valuable time had to be spent explaining why needs cannot be met.

The Report confirms the often stated truism that good community care, if it is to provide the services and support to enable people to live as independently as possible, is not a cheap option. The example it gives is of a district home care service for 130 people with learning difficulties. This involved ninety people providing care for a cost of £50,000 a year, two and half times more than the £20,000 a year estimated for institutional care. The results of this however were reflected in the response of one man living in a shared tenancy household that 'It's blooming great, actually', who according to the hospital resettlement officer had previously 'led a life of complete misery in the community'.

The individual accounts are sensitively discussed, with powerful and often moving contributions from all those involved in care, with the central place given to users themselves. Users describe how they have sought to live independent and fulfilling lives sometimes with the encouragement of official agencies, and sometimes despite them. There are no pat solutions offered and the Report often comes to discomforting conclusions, for example there is no evidence on the basis of their present organisation, that publicly provided services are necessarily always better than those offered by the private sector.

In tracing the response of agencies and professionals, resource shortages were identified as a significant problem, but the way that needs are assessed also figured in the responses of users. For example, a young woman who had been born with Spina Bifida felt that she knew what she needed and that she was being patronised rather than empowered by an assessment undertaken by an occupational therapist. She objected to being asked to perform specified physical tasks as part of an assessment:

It's as if I'm a liar and don't know what I need. I've been telling her, and filling in these forms.

Another woman with physical disabilities disputed the care package that was put together for her involving district nurse support and home care following hospitalisation. She eventually found out through her own informal network that she could buy her own package of care from a private agency with financial help from the Independent Living Fund. She praised her social worker for helping to facilitate this wish by 'cutting through the red tape'. The Report illustrates the dilemmas this involved. While the user was very pleased the agency provided carers who were paid at an hourly rate significantly lower than that paid to (already low paid) council workers. They also received no sick pay or holiday pay.

The social worker was also identified as helpful by an older woman who wished to leave hospital and return to her sheltered flat after having broken her hip for the second time. Against the advice of hospital staff she went home with the help of a package of care which involved a team of home carers ('intensives') providing her with personal and domestic care sufficient to make a success of her decision to leave hospital.

The few examples I have given from the Report should be sufficient to show that it repays detailed study. It points clearly where further research needs to go in this area, and could serve as an extremely useful educational and political tool for joint discussions of groups of users, carers, providers, managers and politicians, in the struggle to construct a progressive alliance in community care. Though sympathetic to the financial plight of local authorities, and acknowledging the progress made, the Report also lends support to the idea that considerable change and empowerment of users is also necessary, and that a flexible, integrated and 'seamless' service remains in most instances an ideal rather than a reality. It shows how the circumstances, and also the needs and wishes of users are often diverse, supporting the shift to individualised services. At the same time NALGO sought to confront the immediate organising dilemmas for trade unions by organising a seminar of branches, which led to the issuing of a handbook for branches, which was more defensive in tone and approach (NALGO, 1993).

The challenge for the future is to find ways of bringing together approaches which combine opposition to the negative effects of government policies and defence of the rights of paid workers, with campaigns to develop and extend progressive possibilities for needs based, participative services. The final example of union sponsored research, the COHSE/MIND *Guidelines for Empowering Users of Mental Health Services*, seek to do just this. Written by two users of services, Jim Read and Jan Wallcraft (1992), with considerable experience of establishing user groups, they represent a radical new departure for the trade union movement. The Guidelines do more than seek the views of users on the services they receive. They go on to ask for help and advice on how to redress their negative effects in ways that promote the empowerment of users. The Preface, by Hector MacKenzie as General Secretary of COHSE, and Judi Clements as MIND's national director, challenges the inevitability of the 'zero sum' view of power criticised earlier in this chapter, by declaring:

> In helping users empower themselves COHSE can only strengthen itself. MIND and COHSE want to see services in which mental health workers can fully realise their potential by providing users with the mental health services they need and want (p 4).

Or, as Read and Wallcraft put it,

> It is not easy to empower or value others when you do not feel powerful and valued yourself (p 5).

This new approach undoubtedly has broader implications for community care and indeed the public services as a whole. The Guidelines show how it is possible, despite the difficulties, to construct a principled partnership between workers and users, linking the organisations which represent them in a new and potentially powerful 'community care alliance'. One immediate effect of this has been formal recognition of the Guidelines by the Department of Health as a basis for developing schemes of user involvement in mental health services.

Read and Wallcraft start by charting the rise of user movements in mental health showing that though it has deep historical roots, it really took off the 1960s and '70s, 'the era of social protest and liberation'. Thus the shift to acknowledgement of user rights has been campaigned for from below by users and radical professionals, and has not been simply generously granted from above by legislative measures such as the 1986 Disabled Persons Act and 1990 Community Care Act. They then provide an extremely useful guide to the variety of types of self advocacy at local and national level which has developed since the mid-1980s, before outlining their philosophical approach. They side with widespread criticisms of the medical model within the user/survivors' movement, for its tendency to break down complex life problems into sets of standardised symptoms and diagnoses (p 8). This 'medical framework' then takes power away from users and often adds to their problems. They argue that it doesn't get to the root causes of mental health problems, and seeks to suppress symptoms in the name of a male, Eurocentric, heterosexual, able-bodied, middle- or upper-class view of normality. They then substantiate some of the ways this occurs through treatments which involve passivity and compliance, for example through imposed drug treatment, lack of information about rights and choices, labelling, poor facilities and pressure to comply with institutionalised regimes.

By talking to COHSE members they came to the conclusion that this has been reinforced by the way that the system treats mental health workers within a 'Cinderella' service. Underfunding and lack of management support are compounded by lack of suitable training, decent treatment from employers, and opportunities to speak up for users 'without fear of criticism or victimisation'. If anything the situation that they highlight is getting worse. A pronounced shift is occurring from the 'pluralist' managerialism which developed in the health and social services in the 1970s as a result of union pressure and favourable employment legislation, and which recognised workers loyalties to their work groups and unions, towards an increasingly 'unitary' managerialism. This demands obedience to managerial leadership, often in competition with union and work group loyalty, and is reinforced by the emphasis on secrecy that is associated with competitive contracting. COHSE has argued that this is creating 'a climate of fear' in the health service which has prevented workers speaking out on the issue of standards of care. Read and Wallcraft found that workers who tried to use the UKCC Code of Professional Ethics to say that ward conditions were unsafe for patients, had been threatened with disciplinary action. Despite this, some 'whistle blowers' like Graham Pink and others have run the risk. Before it became part of UNISON, COHSE had initiated an as yet unsuccessful campaign to give health workers the legal right to raise concerns about standards of care without fear of reprisal. With community care, this now needs to be extended across both the health and welfare services.

The major part of the Guidelines offer advice on how paid mental health workers might empower users. These recognise the constraints that workers often face, but nevertheless say that positive actions can be taken both by the individual worker, and as a union branch. They argue that, among other things, health workers can offer choices rather than impose treatments, can listen and talk to users, and not dismiss complaints and anxieties as symptoms of mental illness. At a more collective level they suggest that user involvement will only work if there is genuine power sharing. This may require the advice of facilitators who are or have been users, and arrangements for acting on users' expressed preferences. They suggest models of good practice for involving users in staff appointments. Echoing the conclusions of the NALGO research discussed above, they argue that good information and publicity is a necessary part of any scheme of empowerment. At an individual level rights can only be safeguarded if people have access to an advocate, and quality assurance mechanisms must have user input.

Their central argument is that empowerment strategies are not an optional extra but integral to the creation of needs based services. This is a point made by other commentators. For example the authors of a survey of attempts to develop needs-based services for people with learning difficulties in Wales show how empowerment strategies for user involvement were crucial to its success, and they argue that this is generally true for community care (McGrath and Grant, 1992).

The three pieces of research discussed above point to the emergence of an ambitious and radical programme of reform in community care, which UNISON and the labour movement could play a leading part in helping to bring into being. They point to the need to do more than campaign against government policies and for increased resources. The NUPE research shows how home carers could be used as a vital resource in community care, in helping to realise the stated aim of enabling people to live as independent a life as possible in their own homes. The NALGO research identifies the diversity of needs and wishes of users and carers of community care, and some of the positive steps that agencies and professionals can take to fulfil them. The COHSE/MIND Guidelines show how it might be possible, given the will, to start empowering users in existing services in ways that also enhance the power and self respect of paid workers. The next chapter seeks to develop the principles prefigured in these and other progressive approaches to identify some basic features of 'good' user centred and worker friendly community care.

# Chapter 6
# So what is good community care?

This chapter proposes some basic principles for 'good' community care, and the wider conditions necessary to make it work which go beyond the limitations of the 1990 reforms. While there may be tensions and difficulties involved in seeking to be both user-centred and worker-friendly, this can be realised within a genuinely pluralist system of community care, which respects and seeks to implement the social rights of all participants: users, carers, and employed workers. This pluralistic service could be implemented in the context of one which was predominantly publicly funded and provided in constructive collaboration with the voluntary sector. It does not need a commercially oriented 'plurality of providers' to bring it into being. The model which informs this chapter, in opposition to the managerialist-consumerist approach, is a socialist ideal of community care as a free association of producers, including the person receiving care, who should as far as possible be in control of the 'labour process', while at the same time respecting the needs and rights of other producers. This is what is meant by 'user-centred and worker-friendly' care. This chapter is therefore not a blueprint, but an attempt to establish an agreed framework for debate within a progressive community care alliance involving unions, user groups, Labour local authorities, voluntary sector groups, and other interested parties. It deliberately leaves open many important and vexed questions, such as the extent and means by which contracting can be turned to positive purposes; how far voluntary organisations should play a central part in mainstream provision; and the precise limits to be set on professional power, carers' responsibility, and user self determination.

## A Shift in Location and Adequate Resources is Only the Start

The first basic principle is that the shift to a community location is a necessary but not sufficient condition for achieving a user-centred service. Also, though it may create some difficulties of transition and present greater challenges for employed workers than the previous system, such a shift is in their interests too. This is because community care creates the preconditions for more satisfying and less custodial forms of work, in the context of an egalitarian and negotiated relationship with users. It thus potentially enhances the skills of employed workers, and alongside this strengthens the claim that they should be properly trained, resourced, and rewarded. It also potentially strenghtens the position in the power structure of those staff, like nurses, home-carers and residential care workers, who have traditionally shouldered care. Many of the same points apply also to lay carers, but we must remember that lay carers, however, are a separate issue, as a shift to community care may well add to their difficulties.

Despite this, the shift to community care is a necessary precondition for the creation of more humane and socially appropriate responses to the needs of users of mental health services, older people, people with learning difficulties, or people with physical disabilities. However it is not sufficient: the second basic principle is therefore that sufficient resources are necessary to make it work. As has often been pointed out, community care is not necessarily a cheap option, and may in fact require more resources rather than less, for two main reasons. First, because custodial hospitals and other institutions, by gathering large numbers of dependent people under one roof, enabled 'economies of scale' to be achieved, even if at the expense of the morale and well-being of those providing and receiving care. Second, unless it is promoted for entirely cynical reasons, community care is often associated with higher expectations of what can and should be done to enhance the quality of life for previously stigmatised and devalued groups of people.

Yet though proper funding and resourcing is a necessary precondition for the creation of good community care, it is even so not enough. We now therefore need to turn our minds to what is meant in specific terms by 'good'. The third basic principle therefore is that user-centred services need to involve more than a shift in location, and the provision of adequate resources, but also a fundamental change in the process by which services are delivered, at both day-to-day and strategic planning levels. Thus good community care will involve a shift away from the justly criticised, bureaucratic and professionally dormant services of the past, which were often insensitive to users' needs. Shifting to the community is more likely to facilitate this change, but will not automatically effect such a result, unless there are conscious efforts to organise services according to different principles. What this also implies is a need for a more general shift in services towards this model, whether in preventive, curative or caring services, whether in institutions or the community. In other words a democratic shift in the social relations of service delivery, of which community care forms just one part.

A few basic conditions for implementing the anti-hierarchical and democratic principles behind community care are laid down here. Above all implementing community care should not be just the province of politicians, planners and bureaucrats, but involve a pluralistic approach to goal-setting and service delivery. As part of this all employed workers should be given greater opportunities to participate in decision making, both individually and through the organisations which give them a collective voice. Lower ranking employees are often those in closest continuing contact with those in need. Not only have they a right to be involved, they have much to contribute to any service genuinely concerned with quality of provision. Many are women, often from black and ethnic minority backgrounds and without paper credentials, but they have acquired caring skills in other settings which are undervalued or even go unrecognised in the public services. There is also often less social distance and more rapport between such workers and users than higher ranking and self important professionals. The breakdowns in communication that occur because of the social distance between professionals and users is a major reason why services fail – though this is not necessarily to argue that professional expertise or authority has no legitimacy at all. In the past the exclusion of lower ranking workers from genuine participation was one of the reasons why custodialism and abuse occurred. While not excusing it, it must be recognised in part as a defensive reaction to forms of hierarchical control which left front-line workers with very little influence on policy, but left them to manage custodial systems with minimal support in extremely difficult and poorly resourced conditions.

The principle of 'worker participation', however, especially as traditionally defined, does not go far enough, for two reasons. First, it restricts itself to employed workers, and needs to be extended to include volunteers and carers. Second, since users themselves have to 'work' at normality, it needs to be extended to embrace user self-determination and self-advocacy wherever feasible. Certainly, research is already beginning to show that in order to empower users in community care, it will also be necessary to empower front line workers within services (eg Onyett and Malone, 1993; Parsloe and Stevenson, 1993). In other words a dual strategy of democratic empowerment will need to be initiated if the full progressive potential of community care is to be realised. This dual strategy is now formally accepted by public service unions, but they have only just begun to think about what it might mean in practice. How far user participation should extend, along a continuum from 'consultation' at one end to 'control' at the other, comes down to a number of fundamental and difficult issues:

- How can the needs and rights of all participants – users, employed and lay carers – be balanced and on what basis should conflicts be resolved?
- Are users always the best judges of their own needs and rights, or in what circumstances should an advocacy or protective role be assumed by others on their behalf?

- What are the circumstances, if any, in which the desire for individuals to ecercise autonomy and self-direction over their lives, should be overridden by employed workers, on behalf of a wider 'social good'? It is much easier to pose these questions than to provide answers, which might not in any case be the same for all groups of users in all sets of circumstances. However, the commitment of any decent system of community care should always be to expand the area of user control and self-direction available. This must include a direct voice in who cares for them, whether as paid workers, relatives or friends.

Of course tensions and conflicts occur not just between users, carers and employed workers. They also occur among different groups of workers, such as between lawyers, managers, nurses, social workers, and doctors, and between them and politicians. Often the conflict is about who shall exercise rights of advocacy, or intervene to guarantee the social good, and on what grounds they should do so. Often these disputes go on without reference to what users might want, even when they are able to express a view. The principle must be established that though different professional groups may have technical expertise this does not necessarily equip them to make ethical decisions on behalf of users. For example, the fact that a surgeon is technically brilliant at sterilising a young woman with learning difficulties, does not make him or her ethically competent to judge whether such a procedure is necessary or not. Thus a pluralistic decision-making structure can be justified on the basis that ethical matters are for humans rather than experts, and if it is also 'user centred' this will in the vast majority of instances be the person directly affected.

Advocacy by others, even with the best intentions, can still render people dependent in positions where they potentially could exercise power, which is why representatives of user groups have increasingly emphasised the possibilities for self-advocacy. Self-advocacy, which emerged out of the self-help movements of the 1960s, may flourish best when users' collective as well as individual voice is recognised (for the principles of self-advocacy see Williams and Shoultz, 1982). This simply means that employed workers should accept that the rights they claim for themselves collectively and individually as trade unionists, must also be extended as a human right to users and carers. This does not prevent either employed or non-employed workers from speaking for themselves, in their own interests. Indeed the more users are able to articulate their own interests, the more workers will be able to clarify their own. What has happened in the past, however, and continues to happen, is that paid workers and carers (not always consciously) have spoken for themselves in the name of users.

This does mean that community care services will need to take into account the legitimate interests of paid workers, volunteers and carers, which will sometimes conflict with those of users. It does not mean that decisions should never be made by paid workers or carers against the wishes of users either to protect them or the wider public from harm. The point is however that services at present do this routinely, to an extent far beyond that which could be rationally justified. Thus the approach advocated here for good community care is defined as 'user-centred' rather than universally 'user led', though in many instances this will be one and the same thing.

The fundamental problem with the consumerism involved in the concept of 'user led' services which lies behind the community reforms is that they fail to confront the reality of power in human service work. First of all, a condition of consumer sovereignty in economic theory is access to full information and ability to act on it. In human service work this will be affected by such factors as type of disability and age, class, gender and 'race', and the reforms fail to acknowledge that additional efforts must be made if an approximate equality between consumers is to be achieved. The second problem with consumerism is that it fails to acknowledge that in many instances decisions will continue to be imposed upon users, not just because of rationing imperatives, but because services in community care will continue in practice to be about community control. This is most explicit in mental health, where government proposals for compulsory community 'parole' make this highly explicit. Therefore the concept of user centredness draws attention to the need for the left to be up-front about the issue of social control. On the whole the left sees this as intrinsically a 'bad thing', but the failure to acknowledge in theory that some form of social control is necessary is one reason why in practice 'actually existing' socialism has been so oppressive. It is time to engage with the user movement on this issue.

At the heart of these community care controversies is a deep questioning of professional powers which in a previous era were regarded as unassailable. Because of the prevailing climate, the neo-liberal right have often been influential in highlighting the 'disabling' effects of professional power, and in calling for its erosion through individual empowerment within a market context (eg Illich, 1977; Szasz, 1972). The alternative to this is not defence of the status quo, but 'radical professionalism' which recognises the need to disperse power to other paid workers, and to empower users individually *and* collectively. Within this model expertise is not a form of 'cultural capital' restricted to professional groups. Nor is it assumed that all problems can be solved by adjustments to individual lives - many require collective political action. Consistent with this is a redefinition of the day to day role of the professional as an 'enabler' who facilitates self advocacy in a working alliance with users. This encompasses, but goes beyond, 'informed consent', to embrace the principles of professional practice which Brechin and Swain called 'shared action planning' (see below). Thus a radical professionalism could accept many of the neo-lib-

## Six principles of professional practice

Brechin and Swain (1989) suggest six principles of practice for professionals wishing to work in alliance with people with learning difficulties – though there is no reason why they could not simply be adopted as good principles of health and social service work, not just in the community, but any setting. According to their principles professional work is:

1. to be an entitlement rather than an imposition;
2. to promote self-realisation rather than compliance;
3. to open up choices rather than replace one option with another;
4. to develop opportunities, relationships and patterns of living, in line with individual wishes rather than rule-of-thumb normality;
5. to enhance users' decision-making and control of their own lives;
6. to allow them to move at their own pace.

They concede that these principles are not necessarily easy to implement in practice.

eral criticisms of traditional professionalism, but would, in place of consumerism, advocate democracy, and alternative enabling strategies which acknowledge dependency and address the social context of personal troubles and problems.

We have seen that it is unrealistic to expect that good community care will simply emerge out of a service structured on pluralistic, worker friendly and user centred lines. There is also a need to subject the objectives of community care to deep questioning and debate. Since the 1970s, the normalisation or ordinary living principle has increasingly been proposed as the dominant goal for community care, and we must therefore focus some attention on it in order to clarify some of the issues already raised.

## The Debate About 'Normalisation'

Normalisation is a clumsy and to a certain extent a misleading name for a radical approach to organising human service work. It seeks to counter the disabling effects of professions and institutions and empower users within services, and it is optimistic about the possibilities for people with disabilities to live an independent and meaningful life with the same choices of lifestyle as are generally available. Normalisation is thus a radical concept with profound implications for restructuring stigmatising and disabling services, in order to enable people to realise their capacities rather than reinforcing their supposed deficits. It is a concept and approach that has been implicitly or explicitly endorsed by recent policy documents developed by UNISON's predecessor unions. For example,

NUPE's recent *Report of the Disability Working Party* spoke of the need for 'putting ability first' and COHSE's *Report on the Future of Services for People with a Mental Handicap* endorsed the influential approach to normalisation elaborated by O'Brien and Tyne (1981).

The concept of normalisation – now sometimes referred to as 'social role valorisation' (SRV) (Wolfensberger, 1983) – cannot however simply be endorsed without further discussion. Its meaning is hotly contested, and has changed over time, and while some of the debate has led to refinement of the original concept, there is no doubt that some of the unresolved disputes reflect political differences among participants to the debate, about such issues as the role of professionals, and how disability is dealt with by the wider society. In addition, some advocate normalisation as the approach to follow, while others seek to confine it within certain limits.

The concept of normalisation originated as a strategy for changing services for people with learning difficulties, but it has increasingly been applied to a much wider range of disabilities. It was first formulated by Bengt Nirje in Scandinavia at the end of the 1960s (Nirje, 1969), but its most influential exponents in Britain and North America have more often followed the approach of Wolf Wolfensberger, first stated in 1972 and reformulated as Social Role Valorisation (SRV) in 1983 (Wolfensberger 1972, 1983). The intellectual antecedents of normalisation were various. The sociological critiques of the negative effects of institutions on people with disabilities, such as Goffman (1961) were one. This emerged out of a growing anti-institutional literature, partly influenced by the revulsion a Nazi concentration camps after the Second World War. Labelling theory with its emphasis on the social construction or reinforcement of deviance

---

## Some basic principles of good community care

1. A shift of services to a community location
2. The provision of sufficient resources
3. A pluralistic structure organised on user centred and worker friendly lines
4. A social rights approach to normalisation strategies
5. Public action to create a community fit to be cared for in
6. Public action to create a community fit to care

and dependence, and heavily critical of the scientific pretensions of the biomedical model of disability, was another sociological influence (eg Scheff, 1966). The influence of the humanistic psychology of, among others, Maslow (1973) and Rogers (1978), with their emphasis on universal human developmental needs and potentialities for 'self-actualisation', can also be detected. What was distinctive about normalisation, however, was its potentially positive role not just as a means of analysing and criticising, but also of changing the way services were organised. As Tim Robinson puts it, even though he is critical of some of the implications of the concept, normalisation for people with learning difficulties was a tremendous step forward in that it:

> added force to the rediscovery of optimism and to the attack on a hundred years of underestimation of their potential (Robinson, 1989, p.247).

This renewal of optimism has now spread across the whole sphere of disability. Despite problems with the concept, it has stood the test of time, and though there may be a certain amount of hype associated with normalisation, there are good reasons for believing that the grounds for optimism are basically genuine.

Though there is common ground between them, proponents of normalisation stem from two traditions, the Scandinavian and Anglo-American, each with a different political emphasis. The Scandinavian tradition associated with Nirje places a much greater priority on its possibilities for expanding the social rights of people with disabilities, while those in the Anglo-American tradition of Wolfensberger appear to temper this with integrationist concerns (Brown and Smith, 1992). One danger is that this can easily end up as a newer, if softer, form of professional dominance and even social control over people with disabilities.

Thus Nirje's definition of normalisation places at the centre the notion that the rights available to people in wider society should also be available to people with learning (and by implication other) disabilities. Thus he saw it as:

> making available patterns and conditions of everyday life which are as close as possible to the norms and patterns of the mainstream of society. An ordinary life includes a normal rhythm of days, weeks and years, normal-sized living units, adequate privacy, normal access to social, emotional and sexual relationships with others, normal growing-up experiences, the possibility of decently paid work, choice and participation in decisions affecting one's future (Nirje, 1969).

Wolfensberger did much to develop this principle as a practical tool. Shifting the attention away from de-hospitalisation and desegregation as an end in itself, he argued that normalisation was a 'universal guiding principle' appropriate to all human services, but that it 'is especially powerful when applied to services to people who are devalued by the larger society' (Wolfensberger and Tullman, 1989). The aim is to reduce differentness and stigma in two ways. First, by seeking to challenge the negative stereotyping of the wider society regarding 'devalued' persons. Second, by enhancing the self-image and social competence of devalued persons, to assist them to participate in 'socially-valued roles' — hence the emphasis on 'social role valorisation'. Cutting through the jargon, this means that normalisation seeks to ensure the full social and not just physical integration of people with disabilities into society.

Both approaches are a significant step forward from previous segregative and 'deficit'-based approaches. However Nirje (1989) and others have argued that Wolfensberger seems concerned to secure compliance from disabled people to existing social norms as the price for integration, rather than advocating social participation for groups of devalued people on their own terms. Particularly controversial has been his emphasis on what he calls the 'conservative corollary' to normalisation which appears to suggest that people with learning difficulties must make extra efforts to gain social acceptance:

> Thus it is not enough for a human service to be merely neutral in either diminishing or enhancing the status of devalued persons in the eyes of others; it must seek to effect the most positive status possible for its clients. For example, on occasions where either a suit and tie or a sports jacket and sports shirt are equally appropriate attire, the man at value-risk in society would fare better wearing the suit-and-tie combination (Wolfensberger and Tullman, 1989).

As critics have pointed out, this puts the onus on people with disabilities to make themselves as inconspicuous as possible, rather than exercise assertive choices that might increase their visibility in able-bodied society, but not immediately enhance their acceptability.

This issue is associated with another criticism, often made of 'strong' versions of labelling theory, that they seek to wish away the existence of disability, in seeing 'differentness' as produced solely by the social labelling process. In so doing, it is argued, real and pressing needs may go unacknowledged, and unrealistic expectations of self-reliance placed on people with disabilities. Campaigners within the disability movement by contrast, have campaigned for the right to be different and equal (Morris, 1991).

Approaches based on normalisation are not without critics. It is sometimes argued that normalisation is only appropriate for mild forms of mental or physical disability, a view just as strenuously denied by proponents (Perrin and Nirje, 1989). Sometimes it is felt in rather despairing terms that the wider society is so irredeemably unaccommodating that disabled people might often be better off in a safe haven or genuine asylum or colony, for example the L'Arche communities, or Geel in Belgium (Sedgwick, 1982; Robinson, 1989). Others oppose colonies but despite this argue the need for genuine temporary asylum in the community, which would restore 'asylum' to its original meaning as 'place of safety' rather than 'place of confinement' (Socialist Health Association, 1989).

Thus the fourth principle of good community care is a 'social rights' approach to normalisation, informed by the 'underlying values' advocated by Shulamit Ramon (1991b):

People first
Respect for persons
Right to self-determination
Right to be dependent
Empowerment

The right to be dependent is included in this list since there is a danger that neoliberalism could mean that *independence* be enforced in future.

Seen in this light, the issue of separate living, and the extent to which people wish to lead lives autonomously of professional help, must be left for people with disabilities to resolve for themselves. However this does not absolve able-bodied people from the political responsibility to create services which do not deter people with disabilities, and forms of social life which facilitate rather than place obstacles to social participation. This is the logic of a social rights approach which sees community care as an extension of choice, rather than an imposition. Thus Gillian Dalley (1988) argues strongly that older people should have a social right to good residential care. Choice also involves the choice not to live in the bosom of the family.

## The Wider Conditions for Good Community Care

Fiona Williams (1989b) suggests that in common with other oppressed groups like women and black people, people with disabilities face three political options:

integration into the world as it is;
withdrawal into a separate culture;
enter the world and change it.

The more radical approach to normalisation will increasingly facilitate the third strategy she outlines. In adopting this challenging stance social movements of devalued people are daring to demand equal treatment, and more, to challenge what 'ordinary living' means in a disablist and healthist society. Rather than accept the same hierarchical and competitive principles as the wider society, widening the rights of people with disabilities will thus mean changing society for the benefit of other people disadvantaged by class, 'race' and gender.

One problem with a social rights approach might be an implicit assumption that self-actualisation is available to most people through 'ordinary living'. In fact opportunities to realise choice and autonomy are strongly structured by social divisions of class, gender and 'race', and how these affect experiences of education, employment, unemployment and housing. One must therefore always look at the wider social context in which normalisation is to be implemented. It is no accident that the more progressive Scandinavian version originated in a society with a strong emphasis on rights to social welfare (Robinson, 1989). Linked to this, we must recognise that though mental health service users, or older people, or people with learning difficulties share a common set of oppressions or disadvantages in relation to the wider society, not all their interests or needs are homogeneous. These will vary according to the nature and degree of their impairment, and also be affected by social divisions of class, 'race' or gender. Approaches based on the need to individualise services may recognise differences of need based on impairment, but generally miss or seriously underestimate the significance of interaction between impairment and wider social divisions.

This leads on to another issue, that good community care needs a favourable social environment. This then is the fifth basic principle, that good community care needs public action to create a community fit to be cared for in. In other words community care can facilitate the creation of a society which places much less emphasis on a 'common lifestyle' but more on enabling its citizens to make their own choices about how to direct their lives in diverse directions. This is to challenge the conservative discourse of community care produced during the Thatcher era, based on a restrictive notion of normality and normal living which demands increasing conformity of all subordinated social groups to the requirements of a white, male and class-dominated society; for example, a society which now insists by law that, among other things, sex education must be taught in the context of 'family values', that local authorities may not 'promote' gay and lesbian sexuality as 'normal', and that single parent families are to be frowned upon, especially when they are headed by women who choose to live without men. This is not the kind of society in which genuinely pluralistic community care can flourish, but rather restricts its horizons to those which obey more ruthlessly applied market and social disciplines.

Thus 'good' community care must also question the narrow restrictions allowed within socially imposed definitions of normality. In the words of Franco Basaglia, one of the leading figures of the Italian Psychiatrica Democratica movement:

It must be emphasised, in case any confusion on this point still remains, that what is proposed here is not mere tolerance of mental illness, as the alternative to suppression. When the mentally ill are no longer segregated – conceptually as well as spatially – we are forced to recognise their peculiarities and at the same time discover our own: for 'normality' can be just as much a distortion as madness. Only if relationships with the 'sick' person are maintained unbroken can his fellows (sic) continue to recognise him as one of them, and to identify their own needs with his (Franco Basaglia, in D Ingleby (ed), 1981, p.192).

The bosom of the family needs all the support it can get.

Thus 'good' community care should not solely focus on people with disabilities themselves, and help them to refashion themselves in terms more acceptable to the existing society. It must take seriously the claim of movements of physically disabled people, that though 'impairment' and 'disability' may be problems experienced by the person, 'handicaps' are problems imposed by society's restrictions. The World Health Organisation makes the following distinctions in the 1980 International Classification of Impairments, Disabilities and Handicaps (ICIDH); underlying the social source of problems experienced by people with disabilities;

IMPAIRMENT: parts or systems of the body that do not work
DISABILITY: things people cannot do
HANDICAP: social and economic disadvantages
(*Source* Lonsdale, 1990, p.20)

If social pluralism means anything, it also means taking serious steps to refashion society to make it more acceptable to people with disabilities. This does not mean abandoning all therapeutic goals. The distinction must be made between the reality of 'impairment' and the socially-imposed nature of 'disability'. Impairment signifies that something has been lost, which it would have been better to prevent, or restore. This does not necessarily support a healthist ideology which devalues, stigmatises and marginalises people with disabilities. Some people with disabilities would object to this statement on the grounds that it idealises health, and accepts a stigmatising deficit model of disability. It is indeed a fine line to draw, but there is also a danger of romanticising disability in ways which reinforce the 'triumph over adversity' ideology of a disablist society. Thus I would still argue that in all the emphasis on care, the emphasis on prevention, treatment and rehabilitation can easily be lost, or be seen as not politically valid. One reason for the shift to community care is diminishing expectations of what curative medicine can do for growing numbers of people. Some of this involves a welcome scepticism of over-inflated professional claims, and for long overdue reordering of priorities towards caring services. However there are other agendas, including an attempt to get people to lower their expectations of public services, which is part of an attempt to control costs. An excessive focus on care can also deflect attention away from the need for a community strategy to prevent physical and mental disabilities, whose causes often lie in class, 'race' and gender inequalities (eg Townsend, Davidson and Whitehead, 1988; Cochrane, 1983). Strategies for both rehabilitation and prevention of disabilities raise significant issues which have been highlighted by people with disabilities. It is argued that a one sided emphasis on rehabilitation can place enormous pressure on people with disabilities to conform to the norms of the dominant able bodied society, sometimes at the behest of carers. The debate around the controversial treatment of conductive education for people with cerebral palsy has provided a focus for these concerns (see Finklestein et al, 1993). Strategies for prevention raise complex ethical and political issues when they involve resort to abortion or genetic screening which, allied to innovations in medical technology, create alarming prospects of developing new forms of social Darwinist eugenics, which also generally devalue and even threaten the position of disabled people in society (Oliver, 1990, p 55; Morris, 1991, Ch 3). These are complex and difficult issues; my main aim here is to identify them, so that they can be debated within the context of a broad community care alliance which places users' interests at the centre.

The final difficult issue I therefore want to raise concerns the role of carers, whose social rights may in some instances be in conflict with the social rights of recipients to care. An important principle ought to be that the state should not seek to impose a discriminatory 'duty to care', usually on female partners or daughters, but should facilitate a plurality of patterns of care from full residential care to shared care, the role of the state being to mediate between carers and users seeking to resolve conflicts in a user-centred and worker-friendly way. It also means facing up to the fact that as work, care may sometimes be rewarding, but may also be regarded a 'burden' (Braithwaite, 1990; Perring, 1989; Parker, 1990). In arguing this one must, however, be sure also to recognise the rights and interests of those needing care. Concern with carers has often obscured the needs of users (Morris, 1991, Chs 3, 6; Morris 1991/2). These assertions must be regarded as no more than opening salvos in the debate about the overlapping and conflicting needs and rights of users and carers. However, they do serve to reinforce the fact that the sixth principle of good community care is concerted public action to facilitate the creation of a community able and

## The Carers' Charter

In 1989, a 'Carers' Charter' was drawn up and endorsed by organisations that represent carers. The plan was published in *A New Deal for Carers* by Ann Richardson, Judith Unell and Beverley Aston.

### The Carers' Charter

1. Recognition of their contribution and of their own needs as individuals in their own right;
2. Services tailored to their individual circumstances, needs and views, through discussions at the time the help is being planned;
3. Services which reflect an awareness of differing racial, cultural and religious backgrounds and values, equally accessible to carers of every race and origin;
4. Opportunities for a break, both for short spells (an afternoon) and for longer periods (a week or more), to relax and have time to themselves;
5. Practical help to lighten the tasks of caring, including domestic help, home adaptations, incontinence services and help with transport;
6. Someone to talk to about their emotional needs, at the outset of caring, while they are caring and when the caring task is over;
7. Information about available benefits and services as well as how to cope with the particular condition of the person cared for;
8. An income which covers the costs of caring and which does not preclude carers taking employment or sharing care with other people;
9. Opportunities to explore alternatives to family care both for the immediate and the long-term future;
10. Services designed through consultation with carers, at all levels of policy and planning.

willing to provide informal care, without incurring the costs and disadvantages it currently entails. A central feature of this will be a pluralistic structure of community which mediates potential and actual conflicts of interests between carers and users in a user centred way.

A more pluralistic structure of the kind envisaged here would enable carers to articulate their mixed feelings, would recognise that caring is skilled and difficult work, and acknowledge conflicts of interests and find ways of working through them. This can of course be helped by particular initiatives to support carers, some of which are already happening, for example, the *Support for Carers* document produced by Yorkshire Regional Health Authority. Carers' organisations have themselves developed charters and started pressing their rights. As these show, care in the community is not enough, and it needs combining with more extensive forms of social support in the community. This in turn will not happen unless it is also associated with a fundamental review of what counts as socially valued and productive work in our society (Brotchie and Hills, 1991). As feminists have pointed out, caring in both the public and private spheres has been demeaned, and socially and economically devalued, because it has traditionally been associated with the emotional and physical labour that women are expected to just do as part of their household and family responsibilities, as a reward in itself (eg Graham, 1983). However, we must not forget that self-care also involves the expenditure of physical and emotional labour, part of which involves handling one's own dependency in relation to others.

Britain's membership of the European Community has only curtailed some of the grosser forms of sex discrimination, such as the exclusion of married women from claiming Invalid Care Allowance, and the Labour Party has recognised the need for proper carers' allowances. A more radical approach still would be to restructure the whole social security system in such a way that might break down the distinction between paid and unpaid work. Some advocates of a Basic Income Guarantee (BIG) favour it on these grounds, so long as it is set at a realistically high rate (i.e. much higher than that proposed by the Liberal Democrats' 1992 election manifesto). Whether such a policy is adopted or not, it remains the case that community care can not be isolated – as the 1990 reforms assume – from other areas of social policy. Thus an anti-poverty strategy addressing issues such as income, employment, and housing is a necessary corollary of good community care, in the interests of both users and carers.

## Conclusion: Redefining Community Care

Some have argued that community care is such an elastic concept, whose predominant meanings have so changed over time, that the term ceases to have any useful meaning. It is easier to define it in negative terms as care outside a hospital than to say positively what it entails. The approach taken here is that location is only one part of the definition, but that community care means different things within different political discourses.

In terms of location, the most renowned distinction of course is between on the one hand care in the community, which is defined as the formal care provided by the state and professional groups, whether domiciliary (home-based), day, or 'homely' residential care; and on the other informal care provided by the community, whether kin, friends, neighbours, and sometimes, self-care (Bayley, 1973). Of course both types are always to be found, but even in the 1950s and '60s (and even before the shift from institutional to community care occurred), care in the community was always the socially predominant form. Nevertheless, since the mid-1970s the emphasis in definitions has increasingly been on care in the community, with formal care increasingly defined as playing the supportive rather than the central role. This can be charted through changes in official definitions, for example from that favoured by the Percy Royal Commission on the Law Relating to Mental Illness in 1957, to that put forward by the Royal Commission on the NHS in 1979 (Carpenter and Williams, 1993).

Definitions of community care therefore never simply describe, but always have a political dimension, and underlying this lie different sets of values about an 'ideal' form of community care. The earlier one was linked to a social democratic vision in which the state and professions were very much in charge. The latter version is strongly influenced by the new right, in which the commercial and voluntary formal care is idealised over that of the state, but informal family care is seen as best of all. In other words, notions of community care are always embedded in an implicit or explicit set of ideal social relationships of care. Thus 'good' community care should only in part be defined as therapeutic and other forms of help provided by either professionals or informal carers in the community. These are rather means to an end, which is the civil and social right for people to a lifestyle which is as close to 'ordinary living' as possible, including a high degree of choice and self-direction over one's life. Another radical implication is that to become a reality, this approach to community care requires what Alan Walker (1982) calls care for the community, public provision of benefits, housing, employment and other services and policies without which people with disabilities are likely to live a segregated life in the community if not in an institution. This also focuses attention on the way in which the wider society is organised to make it difficult for people with disabilities, thereby socially constructing various forms of disability and dependency.

All this makes 'good' community care a highly politicised and radical objective, with far-reaching implications not just for the health and social services, but for the way that society is currently organised. In essence it defines community care as an extension of 'citizenship rights', and seen in this light was implicit in the underlying values inherent in the creation of the welfare state. As T H Marshall (1950) pointed out, the creation of the welfare state after 1945 implied an extension of existing civil liberties and political rights to also include social rights to a decent standard of living and way of life. Critics have pointed out not only that this was not intended as a radical assault on social inequalities, but also that there was differential access to these social rights depending on class, 'race', nationality and gender (Williams, 1989a). Community care was in similar terms an implicit promise of the welfare state, in two ways. First, if we define citizenship and indeed 'relative poverty' in terms of access to the means to participate in the lifestyle commonly accepted as necessary in a given society (eg Townsend, 1979), then this ought to imply providing the extra services and resources necessary for people whose disabilities make this a particularly challenging prospect.

A second aspect of community care as citizenship is its emphasis on extending civil rights to people who are denied them, either by oppressive laws, oppressive services, or both of these. The shift to community care should therefore always involve an attempt to move to an anti-oppressive service in an appropriate anti-discriminatory legal framework. I have deliberately included civil rights as part of citizenship, because in Marshall's formulation social rights were seen as a logical extension, which built on top of civil rights. Unfortunately the subsequent debate about the welfare state, including community care, has often been polarised in terms of civil versus social rights. Partly this is because the welfare state itself implemented social rights in a bureaucratic and professionally-dominated form, which new right critics were able to exploit on civil rights grounds. This problem is the source of much of the new right's emphasis on consumerism in health and welfare.

Social democratic and even left-wing responses to the libertarian-inspired critique of institutions have on occasions, particularly in the mental health sector, argued that the attack, either deliberately or unwittingly, justified the removal of social rights to any services (eg Jones, 1972; Sedgwick, 1982). This may be true in particular instances such as the approach taken by Thomas Szasz (1961, 1972), but in general the failure of the British welfare state to respond adequately by constructing a form of community care which extended both civil and social rights created the vacuum in which new right and anti-welfare versions of community care prospered. The ground was thus laid for the Griffiths reforms to pose as the libertarian alternative to professionalism and socialism.

Looked at in this way, the implementation of 'good' community care is not something that can occur without much wider social and economic change, that would encompass much more than a shift in location of services. Without wishing in a book like this to be too programmatic, this would include an extension of anti-discrimination policies, a radical reform of mental health and disability law, and an extension of social rights in the spheres of basic income, employment, housing, transport and education. It would also require a thorough democratisation of public services, the creation of a proper resource base for local government, the integration of health, social services and perhaps also social security administration within a revitalised local government, close regulation of standards in all sectors of care, and a nationally-established framework of rights and liberties for people who need community care services. It also requires us to redefine citizenship in ways that strip it of its conformist associations, to mean the right and socially-guaranteed means to choose a variety of socially-sanctioned lifestyles. In other words, the right to 'work at normality' in our own chosen and diverse ways.

Herein lies both a fundamental contradiction, but also a radical possibility, at the heart of the 'new politics' of community care. The emphasis it places on 'ordinary life' assumes that self-direction and self-fulfilment are the norm in able-bodied society, and behind this lies the mythological view of society as a collection of free and autonomous individuals, whose possibilities for self-fulfilment are in their own hands. But ordinary life for the majority in Thatcher's and now Major's Britain is at best a set of dull compulsions around work, family and community, and a place where increasing numbers struggle to barely survive in a declining capitalist economy. A socialist politics of community care must therefore seek not just to make ordinary living available to all on the not very attractive existing terms, but also to change radically the conditions under which ordinary life is itself led. And this will require substantial public intervention on a wide number of fronts to correct the tendency of the market to privilege some at the expense of the majority.

# Conclusion
# How to get there from here

sAlternative visions of the future of community care are one thing, but how are they to be realised in difficult economic and political circumstances? In the short run, there is undoubtedly a steep hill to climb, for a number of reasons. First, the government itself recognises that there is a gap between the rhetoric and reality of its own reforms. That is why they have in recent statements been seeking to dampen down expectations of what will be available in the wake of the full implementation of the reforms after April 1993. They have also been busy circularising local authorities asking them to collaborate in a watering down of the reforms, by not registering assessments of need in such a way as might lead to legal claims for entitlement. In other words, they are worried that they have constructed a more radical agenda on community care than they feel able or willing to fulfil. Second, many local authorities themselves, as well as being strapped for cash, have on the whole been slow to change their structures to accommodate to the progressive features of the reforms, such as the emphasis on assessing need, and user involvement in the planning and delivery of services. Third, the wider context for realising the progressive features of the community care reforms is not particularly hopeful. In the 1950s and 1960s community care was facilitated not just by a more favourable political climate, but by an economically buoyant labour market which assisted the social inclusion of previously marginalised groups. Slump and mass unemployment in the 1990s are likely by contrast to heighten processes of social exclusion and marginalisation, which will hit the weakest members of society hardest. At the same time the failure of the Tories' economic miracle has produced a fiscal crisis that is encouraging the right to mount a frontal assault on universal social welfare which includes an attack on pension entitlements (No Turning Back Group, 1993). This was confirmed by the shift to the right at the Tory Party Conference in the Autumn of 1993. The particular threat that this poses for people with disabilities has already been prefigured in John Major's recently stated desire to rein in the 'over generous' granting of invalidity benefit, by tightening tests of eligibility. Other measures, such as the ending of government support for employers' sick pay schemes, are likely to make people with disabilities more rather than less vulnerable.

## Towards a 'Third Wave' of Community Care Reform

For all these reasons and also because, as we have seen, the reforms have failed to tackle fundamentally the artificial division between health and social care, 'transitional management' as Hunter (1993b) calls it, will be the order of the day in community care, in which local authorities and health authorities soldier on as best they can, with few illusions about fulfiling a grand plan. Maybe so, but the most important question is, transitional to what? This book has argued that so far there have been two 'waves' of community care reform, both of which have now been beached, partly because they were overtaken by external events. The first wave was restrained by a limited conception of social rights as mediated by bureaucratic and professionally dominant structures, and petered out in the recession and fiscal crisis of the mid 1970s. The second wave of community care has been stymied by its managerial-consumerist approach, and has effectively been beached by the deeper fiscal and economic crisis of the 1980s.

Nevertheless, despite all these problems, the renewal of optimism associated with the shift from a medical to a social model of community care, in which services are tailored to individual needs, is to a large extent an irreversible change in the political landscape. Hence it is not entirely wishful thinking to imagine that even as the second wave of community care reform is diminishing, a third wave is beginning to rise on the crest of an emerging progressive alliance of progressive politicians and voluntary organisations, paid workers, carers and users. The hope is that this time it will gather greater momentum and not prematurely fade. To be successful, this book has argued, such a movement must find ways of managing the conflicting interests of those involved in producing care, while placing the needs and wishes of users at the centre. It must also link into a broader campaign for political change, to secure the social and economic policies that both address the long term problems of the British economy and fulfil people's social needs and aspirations. These must address the unbalanced bias towards finance capital that produced the Thatcher bubble of the 1980s, and involve a shift towards strengthening Britain's severely weakened industrial base. However the need also to invest in people's well being and to recognise the contribution of diverse forms of informal work, including caring, within a broadened and humanistic concept of national wealth, must not be overlooked. In other words, the third wave of community care reform will need to be part of a wider programme of social and economic reconstruction, in which social and economic policies combine to create a genuinely enabling society, after more than a decade of Toryism which, after all, has been a war waged in the name of monetarist dogma against the people of this country.

This growing movement will need nurturing now, if it is to blossom later. Of course trade unionists will need to defend the rights of employed workers at a time when the shift to so called 'user led' services is part of a central government directed initiative to control costs and enforce privatisation, putting local councils under pressure to improve services at the expense of employed workers pay and conditions. However there are spaces in which it will be possible to find ways of maximising what positive features exist in the reforms to take the emerging approach to community care forward. The Labour Party's discussion document produced in April 1993, *New Directions in Community Care* makes a number of suggestions which might be a starting point for local and national activity. It starts appropriately from the viewpoint that community care is essentially 'a human rights issue' which needs to be backed up by legal rights for services to enable people to live independently, as does Sweden's 1988 Care of the Elderly Act. In the absence of these, it calls on local councils to register unmet need, rather than cooperate with government encouragement to water down assessment procedures under the Act, in case they lead to legal action by users to obtain 'entitlements'. It calls also for more 'innovative' approaches to community care, which offer genuinely decentralised forms of control to users and carers, drawing on experiences from a number of local authorities, and a range of care options from independent and semi-independent living, through to individualised provision in permanent residential or nursing care setting. It means ensuring that there is a choice of good quality public services as well as voluntary and private provision.

One of the most difficult dilemmas for the left and trade union movement to confront is the extent to which this admirable objective should be implemented by giving real command over resources to users, including money grants or credits to individuals to purchase care from the market to suit their needs and circumstances. This approach, known as 'service brokerage', has been particularly campaigned for from within the physical disability movement, who have had some experience of working such a system through grants from the Independent Living Fund set up in 1988 (Oliver and Zarb, 1992). It originated in Canada among parents of children with learning disabilities in Vancouver in the mid 1970s, who used it as a means of shifting the bias of provision away from institutional provision to independent living. The 'broker' is compared to a travel agent who arranges individualised packages of care to suit individual needs. It was soon extended to other forms of disability (Brandon, 1991: 157-161). The idea is endorsed as 'exciting' by *New Directions in Community Care*.

For councils anxious to retain political control over services, and trade unions keen to maintain collective bargaining rights and standardised pay and conditions, such a shift in finance and power may appear to be fraught with dangers. From the workers' point of view, there is a danger that such schemes will lead to a deterioration of pay and conditions, fragmentation of career structures and opportunities, and subordination to the whim of users. By rightly focusing singlemindedly on the human rights of users, there is nevertheless the danger of overlooking those of employed workers. In other words there are conflicts of ideology and interest, and a dialogue is only possible on the basis of recognising and accepting they exist.

It might then be justifiable to go on to suggest that users' rights might not be fully guaranteed by a wholesale shift to service brokerage, within a preparedness to look seriously at such proposals, and accept that if they have drawbacks, alternative means must be found of genuinely empowering users. Only then would it be appropriate to suggest that ensuring high standards in the interests of users may not be served by a market free-for-all in which assumptions of individual consumer sovereignty rule. However not all users of services are on an equal footing, and especially in circumstances of limited resources, some groups of 'consumers' may gain at the expense of others, be more able to press their rights than others. In reality powers of brokerage may for groups who find it hard to act as rational, sovereign individuals, be exercised by carers or neighbours. Fragmentation of the market for care might lead less to empowerment than to more abuse and exploitation of users, without any effective system of inspection or accountability. Finally service brokerage can be a means of cash limiting community care and other forms of social provision – which is one reason why right wing pressure groups like the Institute of Economic Affairs are so keen on 'vouchers'. Indeed the creation of the Independent Living Fund in 1988 can be seen as part of the general attempt to cash limit benefits under the 1988 Social Security Act, of which the creation of the cash limited Social Fund to replace payments on the basis of individual need, was another feature.

Thus while schemes of involvement and democratisation which don't give real command over resources may end up changing little, user control over resources and budgets can also have a sting in its tail, and we should therefore not get too carried away in excitement about service brokerage. There are no panaceas.

## In Defence of the State

This does mean, however, that there is a case for retaining a degree of central direction and control within services that shift in a more decentralised direction, in order to make them more responsive to user needs. This implies what Doyal and Gough call a 'dual political strategy' involving the continuance of a strong central authority at national, regional and local levels in order to ensure that considerations of equity are not disregarded (Doyal and Gough, 1991: Ch 14). A socialist strategy for community care would seek to push forward the frontiers of decentralisation, both from central government to the local level, and from the local to the community and individual, in contrast to a government which has often used the mask of decentralisation to increase centralised power. Within agreement on this issue there is of course considerable scope for debate and disagreement, including the proper roles of expert and bureaucratic authority (as defended by Doyal and Gough, see also Doyal, in Bornal et al eds, 1993).

None of this is to argue against much greater decentralisation and individualisation of services, but it is to urge some caution, that there is at least a case to be made for a more than residual degree of central authority. The key, and by no means easy, task then becomes to ensure that central authorities are accountable in ways that they have not typically been in the past. At all times the case for centralised state authority needs to be explicitly justified, rather than assumed.

Within the terms of this continuing debate, in the immediate future the way forward in community care might be for trade unionists, in conjunction with local councils and also the independent sector, to help to initiate small scale 'prefigurative' experiments in genuinely decentralised forms of provision. These are in fact already beginning to take place, and they could then be carefully and honestly evaluated to see the extent to which they ensured good quality user-centred services, while respecting the needs and rights of other 'stakeholders'. These might involve a wide range of schemes which might or might not offer users and/or carers a degree of control over budgets. The 1993 Labour Party Discussion Document commends approaches like the Yorkshire Innovative Practice Learning Network in which the Regional Health Authority seeks to sponsor new forms of good practice from the centre. These various schemes could then be compared with each other and lessons drawn.

One promising route for the future, which might have relevance not just in community care but across the public services, is for trade unionists and local councils to facilitate the emergence of users', workers', and carers' cooperatives. Public sector trade unionists have in the past been suspicious of the creation of trusts, consortia or buyouts, often seeing them at best as 'damage limitation' exercises which will not prevent downward pressure on wages and conditions (NALGO, 1993). However, as an earlier chapter made clear, in community care at least 85 per cent of the care element of transferred funds must be spent in the independent (commercial and voluntary) sector, and it seems appropriate to try to find ways of spending it as imaginatively as possible in ways as far as possible consistent with 'user centred and worker friendly' principles. This does not mean rushing into cooperatives, as to be successful they must be allowed to develop organically from expressed needs (John Goodman, personal communication; Coops Research Unit, 1993).

None of these roads is easy. They all involve seeking to 'work' the new welfare market in community care in as progressive a way as possible, and hence present all kinds of dilemmas and contradictions. Nevertheless it is vital that trade unionists engage with them, rather than simply adopt defensive trade union stances which to outsiders will appear as an unwillingness to shift the balance of power and control in services towards users and carers. By engaging in this way trade unionists will then justifiably demand that employed workers' legitimate interests are safeguarded within a user centred alliance. The creation of UNISON comes at a highly opportune moment for the emergence of a progressive community care alliance forged on these lines. It is in itself a very clear statement that public service workers have decided to speak with one voice, whatever service or rank. In other words, UNISON aspires to create among its own members the basis for a seamless public service. Its philosophy and rules express a firm commitment to quality public services which are accountable to both workers and users. It is therefore only logical that it should seek to realise these goals in the wider world by joining forces with like-minded and campaigning organisations. This is already happening and will continue to happen through one-off campaigns around particular issues. It might also be facilitated by the creation of more formalised umbrella organisations such as a Community Care Alliance committed to clarifying the meaning of, and securing in reality, the reform of community care along user centred and worker friendly lines. As always, then, it is possible to face the future with some degree of confidence and hope, while still being aware that some hard struggles lie ahead.

## Towards Revitalised Public Services

The alternative socialist vision of community care outlined in this book is one that could be applied to the public services generally, involving democratisation instead of privatisation, combined with wider action to create an enabling framework. As far as community care itself is concerned this can be defined in terms of finding the appropriate combination of principles of individualism, familialism and communalism. In the early Thatcher years the shift to community care merely emphasised familialism, that families could and should shoulder care, and that this responsibility should primarily fall on wives and daughters. The Griffith reforms embodied in the 1990 Act departed from this approach to some extent. The Act did, if only in a limited way, acknowledge a communal responsibility to provide support for community care. Its emphasis on individualism recognised in principle the separate rights and interests of users within families, albeit within a consumerist approach, while in a contradictory and more traditionally conservative way continuing to idealise the traditional patriarchal family as a site of care.

The alternative approach to community care advocated here remains strongly attached to principles of communalism, that is citizenship rights and liberties in community care, which are in need of much sharper legal definition. It also argues that the third wave of community care must embrace within this an individualised approach to services, forms of provision which offer lifestyle choices, including who people will be cared for by, consistent with the radical model of normalisation outlined in the previous chapter. It would seek to empower users of services as producers rather than simply consumers of care. Further, rather than imposing a familialist model on carers, it would recognise their rights as individuals to choose to care, and offer facilitative forms of support. At the same time, this progressive alliance would uplift the status, training and rewards available to employed workers, seek to empower rather than subordinate users, and campaign for the wider economic and social changes necessary to support 'good' community care. Above all, it is the failure to recognise that *all* participants in care, as users and waged or unwaged workers, are individuals with both needs for support and skills which need enhancing, that is the root cause of abuse, whether in institutional or community care.

In other words, the aim in launching a third wave of community care is to create a more genuinely 'enabling' state than is dreamt of in Tory philosophies, which both wildly exaggerate the extent to which individuals can overcome social inequality and disadvantage, and grossly underestimate the extent of communal support they need. This is, of course, a long term project, but there is no reason why in the years ahead progressive community care alliances based on user-centred and worker friendly principles can not win some small victories that might propel the third wave forward. There is no doubt that the trade union movement has a crucial role to play in such a movement, but in order to do so it will have to take risks.

# Appendix
# Community care:
# a chronology

## Key developments in the history of state institutions before 1945

**1601 Elizabethan Poor Law**
State sets up institutions for poor and disabled

**1792 York Retreat**
Pioneers 'moral treatment' principles within small asylum serving the Quaker community

**1808 County Asylum Act**
Local authorities empowered to build lunatic asylums

**1832 First Reform Act**
Middle class gain vote

**1834 New Poor Law**
The workhouse defined as the favoured institutional 'solution' to able-bodied poverty but in practice becomes dumping ground for sick and disabled people

**1845 Lunatics Act**
Counties obliged to build asylums for the 'pauper insane', which quickly become large, barrack-like institutions

**1847 Park House**
First 'asylum for idiots' founded in Highgate

**1867 and 1884**
Vote extended to most men

**1890 Lunacy Act**
Emphasis on 'certification' and confinement reinforced

**1908 Old Age Pensions Act**
Non-contributory pensions for 'deserving' older people

**1911 National Insurance Act**
Health and unemployment insurance provided outside poor law

**1913 Mental Deficiency Act**
Institutional 'solution' for people with learning difficulties

**1918 and 1928**

Vote extended to women

**1925 Pensions Act**

State pensions extended to more groups of people but made contributory

**1930 Mental Treatment Act**

Provisions of 1890 Lunacy Act partly relaxed and some mental health 'after care' developed

**1942 Beveridge Report**

Calls for abolition of Poor Law and universal rights to comprehensive social insurance

**1944 White Paper**

General social right to full employment guaranteed

**Disabled Persons Employment Act**

Legal right to work established for people with disabilities

## Key developments in community care 1945-1979

**1945 Labour Government elected**

Implementation of Beveridge Report begins

**1946 National Insurance Act**

Universal social insurance 'from the cradle to the grave'

**National Health Service Act**

Universal and comprehensive health care as a right for all

**1948 5 July**

NHS launched on 'Appointed Day'

**National Assistance Act**

Local authority accommodation for older people, often in former poor law institutions, continues the institutional bias in services for older people

**Children Act**

Community rather than institutional provision endorsed for children in need

**1957 Royal Commission on Mental Illness and Mental Deficiency**

Pronouncement in favour of more liberal laws, under medical authority, and development of community care

**1959 Mental Health Act**

Approach of the 1957 Royal Commission implemented

**1961 Enoch Powell's 'Water Tower Speech'**

Closure of Victorian mental hospitals predicted within fifteen years

**1962 Hospital Plan**

Programme of building District General Hospitals (DGHs) announced, to include acute psychiatric units

**1963 White Paper – Health and Welfare: the Development of Community Care**
Responsibility for care transferred to local authorities, but without earmarked resources
**1967 *Sans Everything* by Barbara Robb**
Cruelty and neglect of older people in long stay institutions exposed
**1970 Chronically Sick And Disabled Person's Act**
Right to services through local authorities established, but without earmarked resources
**1971 White Paper – Better Services for the Mentally Handicapped**
Despite scandals at Ely and other hospitals, only modest encouragement given to community care for people with learning difficulties
**Government Circular – Hospital Services for the Mentally Ill**
Keith Joseph endorses 'medical model' of mental illness, and treatment in District General Hospital psychiatric units rather than traditional mental hospitals
**1974 Labour Government elected**
Radical promises which become compromised by rising economic difficulties caused by 1973 Oil Crisis
**1975 White Paper – Better Services for the Mentally Ill**
Closure of hospitals to be delayed until more resources available for community reprovision
**1976 Labour Government public expenditure cuts**
Pressure from the International Monetary Fund
**DHSS – Priorities for Health and Personal Social Services**
Greater priority to be given to community care and less to acute medicine, but within existing levels of expenditure
**1978 DHSS – A Happier Old Age**
Shift to an increasing emphasis on informal care by relatives heralded, and care *by* rather than *in* the community
**1979 Jay Committee**
Calls for community care and demedicalisation of services for people with learning difficulties

## Key developments in community care since 1979
**1979 Conservative Government elected**
Margaret Thatcher is Prime Minister
**1980 'Amber light' from government**
Social security expenditure to be used to subsidise expansion of private and voluntary but not local authority provision of residential care
**Black Report**
Inequalities in health still pronounced more than thirty years after creation of the NHS

**1981 Care in the Community Initiative**
Closure of mental illness and handicap hospitals accelerated in midst of economic recession
**DHSS Report – Growing Older**
'Informal care' model of community care underlined
**1983 Mental Health Act**
Limited reform of 1959 Mental Health Act, with some additional liberties and shift of power from psychiatrists to social workers
**1985 Banstead Hospital closes**
The first of the Victorian asylums goes
**Report of House of Commons Select Committee on Social Services**
Government criticised for closing mental hospitals without making adequate provision for community care
**1986 Audit Commission – Making a Reality of Community Care**
Calls to reform the 'perverse incentives' to residential care for older people through social security subsidy
**Disabled Persons (Services, Consultation and Representation) Act**
People with disabilities given a right to assessment and a say in provision, prefiguring the wider shift to consumerism in community care
**1987 MIND, COHSE and other pressure groups mobilise**
Criticism of Royal College of Psychiatrists' proposals to introduce compulsory treatment in the community

**Health Divide**
Update of the Black Report by Margaret Whitehead shows that health inequalities are widening
**1988 Griffiths Report – *Community Care: An Agenda for Action***
Recommendation that social security funds be transferred to local authorities to finance 'needs based' community care provision
**1989 White Paper – *Community Care: Caring for People***
Most of the proposals of the Griffiths Report accepted
**Social Security subsidy to residential care tops £1 billion**
**1990 NHS and Community Care Act**
Caring for People implemented, and purchaser and provider functions in both health and social care are split
**1991**
Delay in key financial provisions of the 1990 Act until April 1993
**1992 Government imposed Council Tax Settlement**
Local Authorities plunged into deep financial crisis, threatening wide range of jobs and services
**April 1993 Appointed Day**
Community care reforms come into effect and social security funds start to be transferred to Local Authorities

# References

P Abrams (1984), 'Realities of Neighbourhood Care: The Interactions between Statutory, Voluntary and Informal Social Care', *Policy and Politics*, Vol 12, No 4

P Addison (1982), *The Road to 1945*, Quartet Books

P Aggleton (1990), *Health*, Routledge

J Aldridge and S Becker (1993), *Children Who Care: Inside the World of Young Carers*, Department of Social Sciences, Loughborough University

J Allen (1992), in J Allen, P Braham and P Lewis eds, *Political and Economic Forms of Modernity*, Polity Press

M Allen and C Mather (1992), *Protecting the Community: A Worker's Guide to Health and Safety in Europe*, London Hazards Centre

Alzheimer's Disease Society (1993), *Deprivation and Dementia*

K Amin and C Oppenheim (1992), *Poverty in Black and White: Deprivation and Ethnic Minorities*, Child Poverty Action Group and Runnymede Trust

Y Arai (1993), 'Quality Counts', *Health Service Journal*, 4 March

S Arber and N Gilbert (1989), 'Men: the Forgotten Carers', *Sociology* Vol 23, No 1

P Aries (1962), *Centuries of Childhood*, Penguin

J Askham and C Pharoah (1992), 'Health and Social Care Provision for Older People', *Share*, Issue 3

Audit Commission (1986), *Making a Reality of Community Care*, HMSO

Audit Commission (1992), *Community Care: Managing the Cascade of Change*, HMSO

J Baldock (1989), 'United Kingdom – a Perpetual Crisis of Marginality', in B Munday ed, *The Crisis in Welfare: an International Perspective on Social Services and Social Work*, Harvester

P Barham (1992), *Closing the Asylum: the Mental Patient in Modern Society*, Penguin

R Barn (1990), 'Black Children in Local Authority Care', *New Community*, Vol 16, No 2

M Barnes (1993), 'Introducing New Stakeholders – User and Researcher Interests in Evaluative Research', *Policy and Politics*, Vol 21, No 1

C Barras (1991), *Disabled People in Britain and Discrimination*, Hurst and Company

N Bartlett (1989a), 'The Power to Persuade', *Community Care*, 13 July

N Bartlett (1989b), 'Agreeing to Differ', *Community Care*, 20 July

M Bayley (1973), *Mental Handicap and Community Care*, Routledge and

Kegan Paul

V Beardshaw (1982), *Conscientious Objectors at Work: Mental Hospital Nurses – a Case Study*, Social Audit

P Beresford and S Croft (1981), *Community Control of Social Service Departments*, London: Battersea Community Action

A Bevan (1978) *In Place of Fear*, Quartet

A Bhat, R Carr-Hill and S Ohri eds (1988), *Britain's Black Population: A New Perspective*, Gower, 2nd edition

J Black (1992), *User Involvement: Opening the Door*, unpublished mimeo

Black Mental Health Group (1992), 'Begging for Arrest', *Social Work Today*, 27 February

S Bolger, P Corrigan, J Docking and N Frost (1981), *Towards Socialist Welfare Work*, Macmillan

T Booth (1990), *Better Lives*, Sheffield University

N Bosanquet (1983), *After the New Right*, Heinemann

V Braithwaite (1990), *Bound to Care*, Allen and Unwin

D Brandon (1991), *Innovation Without Change? Consumer Power in Psychiatric Services*, Macmillan

A Brechin and J Swain (1989), 'Creating a "Working Alliance" with People with Learning Difficulties', in A Brechin and J Walmsley eds, *Making Connections: Reflecting on the Lives and Experiences of People with Learning Difficulties*, Hodder and Stoughton

D Brindle (1991), 'Balancing the Social Equation – With Algebra', *The Guardian*, October 9

D Brindle (1992), 'Care in the Community: Task Forces of the Softly-Softly Revolution', *The Guardian*, 8 July

D Brindle (1993), 'Minister Plans to Set up Code of Practice for Social Workers', *The Guardian*, 20 May

J Brotchie and D Hills (1991), *Equal Shares in Caring*, Socialist Health Association

H Brown and H Smith (1992), *Normalisation: a Reader for the Nineties*, Tavistock/Routledge

J M Buchanan and G Tullock (1962), *The Calculus of Consent*, University of Michigan Press

R Bucher and A Strauss (1986), 'Professions in Process', *American Journal of Sociology*, Vol 66

M Bulmer (1988), *Neighbours: the Work of Phillip Abrams*, Cambridge University Press

J Busfield (1986), *Managing Madness: Changing Ideas and Practice*, Unwin Hyman

T Butler (1993), *Changing Mental Health Services: the Politics and the Policy*, Chapman and Hall

B Callaghan, A Coote, G Hulme and J Stewart (1990), *Meeting Needs in the 1990s: The Future of Public Service and the Challenge for Trade Unions*, Institute for Public Policy Research in association with the TUC

M Carpenter (1980), 'Asylum Nursing Before 1914: a Chapter in the History of Labour', in C Davies ed, *Rewriting Nursing History*, Croom Helm

M Carpenter (1988), *Working for Health: the History of COHSE*, Lawrence and Wishart

M Carpenter, R Elkan, P Leonard, and A Munro (1991), *Professionalism and Unionism Among Nurses and Social Workers*, Economic and Social Research Council Report

M Carpenter and F Williams (1993), *Community Care: a Historical Enquiry*, *Open University*, Workbook 2 of Course K259, 'Community Care', Part 1

R Carr-Hill et al (1992), *Skill Mix and the Effectiveness of Nursing Care*, Centre for Health Economics, York

T Chapman, S Goodwin and R Hennelly (1991), 'A New Deal for the Mentally Ill: Progress or Propaganda?', *Critical Social Policy*, Vol 11 No 2

D J Challis and B P Davies (1986), *Case Management in Community Care*, Gower

D Challis et al (1993), 'Case Management in the Care of the Aged: The Provision of Care in Different Settings', in J Bornat et al, eds, *Community Care: a Reader*, Macmillan

T Chandler (1989), 'Community Care: the View from a Union', *Radical Community Medicine*, Spring

L Chester (1992), 'Community Care: Cardboard Box or Prison Cell', *NUPE Journal*, No 6

J Clarke (1988), 'Social Work: the Personal and the Political', Unit 11 of Open University Course D211, *Social Problems and Social Welfare*

M Clarke and J Stewart (1992), 'Empowerment: a Theme for the 1990s', *Local Government Studies*, Vol 18, No 2

D Clode (1992), 'Best Laid Plans', *Community Care*, 30 April

R Cochrane (1983), *The Social Creation of Mental Illness*, Longman

COHSE (1991), *Out of Sight, Out of Mind: COHSE's Evidence to the Residential Staff Enquiry*, Banstead, Surrey

COHSE (1992a), 'Community Nurses: Fight Back or Go Under!', *Health Report*, November, Region 12 (South Yorks and East Midlands)

COHSE (1992b), *The Management of Health and Safety at Work Regulations 1992*

COHSE/NALGO/NUPE in UNISON (1993), *Acquiring Your Rights: A Negotiator's Guide to NUPE and the Acquired Rights Directive*

Commission on Social Justice (1993), *The Justice Gap*

R Common and N Flynn (1992), *Contracting for Care*, Joseph Rowntree Foundation

N Connelly (1988), *Care in the Multiracial Community*, Policy Studies Institute

A Cooke and R Ford (1992), 'Still a Game of Chance,' *Community Care*, 2 July

Coops Research Unit (1993), *Third Sector Care: Manual for Cooperative and Other Small Scale Providers*, Open University

A Coote and N Deakin (1991), *Welfare Beyond the State*, Institute of Public Policy Research

R Crawford (1980), 'Healthism and the Medicalisation of Everyday Life', *International Journal of Health Services* Vol 10 No 3

S Croft and P Beresford (1990), *From Paternalism to Participation*, Open Services Project and Joseph Rowntree Foundation

M A Crowther (1981), *The Workhouse System 1834-1929*, Batsford

G Dalley (1988), *Ideologies of Caring: Rethinking Community and Collectivism*, Macmillan Education

G Dalley (1989), 'Professional Ideology or Occupational Tribalism: the Health Service-Social Service Divide', in R Taylor and J Ford eds, *Social Work and Health Care: Research Highlights*, No 19, Jessica Kingsley Publishers

R Darton and K Wright (1993), 'Changes in the Provision of Long Term Care, 1970-1990', *Health and Social Care in the Community*, Vol 1 No 1

P Day and R Klein (1987), 'The Business of Welfare', *New Society*, 19 June

Department of Health and Social Security (1981), *Care in the Community*, Her Majesty's Stationery Office (HMSO)

Department of Health and Social Security (1983), *Explanatory Notes on Care in the Community*, HMSO

A de Swaan (1990), *The Management of Normality*, Routledge

L Doyal (1993), 'Human Need and the Moral Right to Optimal Community Care', in J Bornat et al eds, *Community Care: A Reader*, Macmillan

L Doyal, G Hunt and J Mellor (1981), 'Your Life in Their Hands', *Critical Social Policy*, Vol 1, No 2

L Doyal and I Gough (1991), *A Theory of Human Need*, Macmillan

P Dressel (1982), *The Service Trap: From Altruism to Dirty Work*, Charles C Thomas, Springfield Illinois

L Eaton (1993), 'Survival of the Loudest', *The Guardian*, 21 April

C Estes (1979), *The Ageing Enterprise*, San Francisco, Josey Bass

M Evandrou, J Falkingham and H Glennerster (1990), 'The Personal Social Services: Everyone's Poor Relation but Nobody's Baby', in J Hills ed, *The State of Welfare: the Welfare State in Britain since 1974*, Clarendon Press

M Evandrou *et al* (1992), 'Equity in Health and Social Care', *Journal of Social Policy*, Vol 21, Pt 4

G Fennell, C Phillipson and H Evers, *The Sociology of Old Age*, Open University Press

S Fernando (1991), *Mental Health, Race and Culture*, Macmillan

V Finkelstein et al (1993), *Disabling Barriers, Enabling Environments*, Sage

M Foucault (1967), *Madness and Civilisation*, Tavistock

M Foucault (1973), *The Birth of the Clinic: An Archaeology of Medical Perception*, Pantheon Press

M Foucault (1977), *Discipline and Punish*, Penguin

D Fraser (1974), 'The Medical Services of the New Poor Law', in D Fraser ed, *The New Poor Law in the Nineteenth Century*, Macmillan

D Fraser (1986), *The Evolution of the British Welfare State*, Macmillan, 2nd edition

E Freidson (1970), *Profession of Medicine*, Dodd Mead

A Fry (1992), 'An Open Door to Abuse', *The Guardian*, 2 December

J Geldeft (1993), 'Workhouse Ethics in Care Provision', *Local Government Chronicle*, 30 April

M George (1992), 'Filling in the Gaps?', *Nursing Standard*, 2 December

V George and P Wilding (1985), *Ideology and Social Welfare*, Routledge and Kegan Paul, 2nd edition

N Ginsburg (1979), *Capital, Class and Social Policy*, Macmillan

C Glendinning (1992), *The Costs of Informal Care*, HMSO

E Goffman (1964), *Stigma: Notes on the Management of the Spoiled Identity*, Prentice Hall

E Goffman (1961) *Asylums: Essays on the Social Situations of Mental Patients and Other Inmates*, Penguin

P Gosling (1992), 'Volunteers Taste Contract Culture', *Independent on Sunday*, 4 October

I Gough (1979), *The Political Economy of the Welfare State*, Macmillan

H Graham (1983), 'Caring: A Labour of Love', in J Finch and D Groves ed, *A Labour of Love: Women, Work and Caring*, Routledge and Kegan Paul

H Graham (1991), 'The Informal Sector of Welfare: a Crisis in Caring?', *So-*

cial Science and Medicine, Vol 32, No 4

H Graham (1993), 'Feminist Perspectives on Caring', in J Bornat et al, eds, *Community Care: A Reader*, Macmillan

J Green (1988), 'General Household Survey 1985', *Informal Carers*, HMSO

R Griffiths (1988), *Community Care: an Agenda for Action*, HMSO

R Griffiths (1992), 'With the Past Behind Us', *Community Care* 16 January

Y Gunaratnam (1993), 'Breaking the Silence: Asian Carers in Britain', in J Bornat et al, eds, *Community Care: A Reader*, Macmillan

J Hadley (1992), *All Change for Carers? Report of One-Day Conference*, Kings Fund Centre

R Hadley and S Hatch (1981), *Social Welfare and the Failure of the State*, Allen and Unwin

C Hallet ed (1989), *Women and Social Service Departments*, Harvester Wheat-sheaf

J Handy (1991), *Occupational Stress in a Caring Profession: The Social Context of Psychiatric Nursing*, Avebury

HEA (1987), *Stress in the Public Sector: Nurses, Police, Social Workers and Teachers*, Health Education Authority

R Hedley and J Davis-Smith (1991), *Volunteering and Society: Principles and Practice*, National Council of Voluntary Organisations

C Hegenbotham (1990), *Return to Community: the Voluntary Ethic and Community Care*, Bedford Square Press

M Henwood (1990), 'Age Discrimination and Health Care', in E McEwen ed, *Age: the Unrecognised Discrimination*, Age Concern

M Hill (1982), 'Professions in Community Care', in A Walker ed, *Community Care: the Family, the State and Social Policy*, Basil Blackwell and Martin Robertson

J Hills and B Mullings (1990), 'Housing: a Decent Home for All at a Price Within Their Means?' in J Hills ed, *The State of Welfare: The Welfare State in Britain since 1974*, Clarendon Press

D Hinchcliffe (1992), 'A Flight Over the Cuckoo's Nest', *Community Care*, 19 March

J Hirst (1993) 'Props for the Welfare State', *The Guardian* 26 May

R Hodgkinson (1967), *The Origins of the National Health Service: the Medical Services of the New Poor Law*, Wellcome Historical Medical Library

D Howe (1986), 'The Segregation of Women and Their Work in the Personal Social Services', *Critical Social Policy*, 15

House of Commons Select Committee on Social Services (1985), *Community Care*, HC 13-1, HMSO

B Hudson (1990), 'A Recipe for Chaos', *Community Care*, 11 October

B Hudson (1992), 'Ignorance and Apathy', *Health Service Journal*, 19 March

R Hugman (1991), *Power in Caring Professions*, Macmillan

D Hunter (1993a), 'To Market! To Market! A New Dawn for Community Care', *Health and Social Care in the Community*, Vol 1 No 1

D Hunter (1993b), 'A Sticking Plaster Job', *Health Service Journal*, 4 March

M Ignatieff (1983), 'Total Institutions and the Working Class: a Review Essay', *History Workshop Journal*, 15

I Illich (1975), *Limits to Medicine*, Penguin

I Illich et al (1977), *The Disabling Professions*, Marion Boyar

D Ingleby ed (1981), *Critical Psychiatry: the Politics of Mental Health*, Penguin Books

Institute of Race Relations (1993), *Community Care: the Black Experience*

M Ivory (1992), 'Labour Plans Funding Shake-up for Voluntaries', *Community Care*, 23 January

N James (1992-93), 'Caring is Hard Work', *Health Matters*, Issue 13

M Jervis (1986), 'Female, Asian and Isolated', *Open Mind*, April/May, No 20

N Johnson (1988), *The Welfare State in Transition: the Theory and Practice of Welfare Pluralism*, Wheatsheaf Books

C Jones (1983), *State Social Work and the Working Class*, Macmillan

G Jones (1986), *Social Hygiene in the Twentieth Century*, Croom Helm

K Jones (1972), *A History of the Mental Health Services*, Routledge and Kegan Paul

K Jones (1988), *Experience in Mental Health: Community Care and Social Policy*, Sage

J Kellet (1993), 'Long Term Care on the NHS: A Vanishing Prospect', *British Medical Journal*, Vol 306, 27 March

J King (1989), 'Promises, but no Guarantees', *Community Care*, 30 November, in Special Supplement on the White Paper, *Caring for People*

King's Fund Centre (1992), *Health and Race*

R Klein (1983), *The Politics of the National Health Service*, Longman

N Korman and H Glennerster (1985), *Closing a Hospital: the Darenth Park Project*, Bedford Square Press/National Council for Voluntary Organisations

Labour Party (1993), *New Directions in Community Care*, Labour Party Discussion Document

H Land (1991), 'The Confused Boundaries of Community Care', in J Gabe et al, eds, *The Sociology of the Health Services*, Routledge

M Langan (1990), 'Community Care in the 1990s: the Community Care White Paper: "Caring for People"', *Critical Social Policy*, Vol 10 No 2

D Leat (1993), *The Development of Community Care by the Independent Sector*, Policy Studies Institute

A Leathard (1990), *Health Care Provision*, Chapman and Hall

I Leedham and G Wistow (1993), 'Just What the Doctor Ordered', *Community Care* 7 January

M Lipsky (1980), *Street Level Bureaucracy: Dilemmas of the Individual in Public Services*, Russell Sage Foundation, New York

J Lister (1991), *Where's the Care? An Investigation into London's Mental Health Services*, COHSE London Region

J Lister (1992), 'Community Care Crisis Looms', *Health Report*, November, COHSE Region 12

Local Government Board (1992), *The Quality of Care: Report of the Residential Staffs Inquiry* (Howe Report)

Local Government Information Unit (1990a), *Caring for People — the Government's Plans for Care in the Community*, Special Briefing No. 32

Local Government Information Unit (1990b), *A Woman's Place is in the Home?*, Community Care Comment: 1

Local Government Information Unit (1992), *The Black Community and Community Care*, Community Care Comment: 2

S Lonsdale (1990), *Women and Disability: the Experience of Disability Among Women*, Macmillan

F Lowe (1992), 'Cut off from Care,' *Community Care*, 27 August

T Lunn (1989), 'Profits or Patients?', *Community Care*, 2 March

L Mackie (1992), *Community Care: Users' Experiences*, NALGO

J Macnichol (1987), 'In Pursuit of the Underclass', *Journal of Social Policy*,

Vol 16, No 3

R Mailly, S J Dimmock and A S Sethi, eds (1989), *Industrial Relations in the Public Services*, Routledge

N Malin (1987), 'Community Care: Principles, Policy and Practice', in N Malin (ed), *Reassessing Community Care*, Croom Helm

T Mallinson et al (1983), *The Future of Psychiatric Services*, COHSE

T H Marshall (1950), 'Citizenship and Social Class', *Citizenship and Social Class and other Essays*, Cambridge University Press

J P Martin (1984), *Hospitals in Trouble*, Basil Blackwell

A Maslow (1973), *The Further Reaches of Human Nature*, Penguin

P Mason (1992), 'Gathering Momentum', *Nursing Times*, 27 May

M McGrath and G Grant (1992), 'Supporting "Needs-Led" Services: Implications for Planning and Management Systems (A Case Study in Mental Handicap Services)', *Journal of Social Policy*, Vol 21, No 1

E J Miller and G V Gwynne (1971), *A Life Apart: A Pilot Study of Residential Institutions for Physically Handicapped and Young Chronic Sick*, Tavistock

K Milne (1993), 'The Dustmen's Contract', *New Statesman and Society*, 23 July

S Milne (1993), 'Binmen Win Sell-Offs Case', *The Guardian*, 31 July

MIND (1992a), *The MIND Guide to Advocacy in Mental Health*, MIND Publications

MIND (1992b), *MIND Manifesto*, MIND Publications

R Moroney (1976), *The Family and the State: Considerations for Social Policy*, Longman

J Morris (1991), *Pride Against Prejudice: Transforming Attitudes to Disability*, Women's Press

J Morris (1991/2), '"Us" and "Them"? Feminist Research, Community Care and Disability', *Critical Social Policy*, Vol 11 No 3

P Morris (1969), *Put Away: a Sociological Study of Institutions for the Mentally Retarded*, Routledge and Kegan Paul

N Murray (1992), 'Anti-racism in Recession', *Community Care*, 30 July

R Murray (1991), 'The State After Henry', *Marxism Today*, May

NAHAT (1992), *Care in the Community: Definitions of Health and Social Care*, National Association of Health Authorities and Trusts, London

NALGO (1985), *Residential Workers' Dispute*

NALGO (1990a), *Care in the Community: Branch Briefing*

NALGO (1990b), *Care in the Community: NALGO Comments on Draft Guidance*

NALGO (1993), *Community Care: Handbook for Local Government Branches*

NUPE (1986), *Time for Justice: NUPE's Report on Care for the Elderly*

NUPE (1990a), *Warding off Wastage: The Case For Equal Opportunities in Nursing*

NUPE (1990b), *A Preliminary Report on the NUPE Home Helps/Home Carers Survey*

NUPE (1990c), *Concerned About Community Care?*

NUPE (1992), *The Workplace Health, Safety and Welfare Relations 1992*

NUPE West Midlands Division and West Midlands County Council (1986), *The Realities of Home Life*

NUPE (1993), *Skill Mix and Reprofiling in the Health Service*, NUPE Guidelines

NUPE/UNISON (1993), *Bringing it all Home: The NUPE Home Care Survey*

B Nirje (1969) 'The Normalisation Principle and its Human Management Implications', in R Kugel and W Wolfensberger eds, *Changing Patterns in Residential Services for the Mentally Retarded*, Washington DC, President's Commission on Mental Retardation

No Turning Back Group (1993), *Who Benefits? Reinventing Social Security*

N North (1993), 'Empowerment in Welfare Markets', *Health and Social Care* Vol 1 No 2

J O'Brien and A Tyne (1981), *The Principle of Normalisation – a Foundation for Effective Services*, CMHERA

M Oliver (1990), *The Politics of Disablement*, Macmillan

M Oliver and G Zarb (1992), *Greenwich Personal Assistance Schemes, an Evaluation*, Greenwich Association of Disabled People Ltd

S Onyett and S Malone (1993), 'Back to Front', *Health Service Journal*, 11 February

A Palmer (1993), 'The Price of Dementia', *The Spectator*, 5 June

G Parker (1990), *With Due Care and Attention: a Review of Research on Informal Care*, Family Policy Studies Centre

R Parker (1990a), 'Elderly People and Community Care: the Policy Background', in I Sinclair, R Parker, D Leat and J Williams eds, *The Kaleidoscope of Care: A Review of Research on Welfare Provision for Elderly People*, HMSO

R Parker (1990b), 'Part Four: Care and the Private Sector', in I Sinclair, R Parker, D Leat and J Williams eds, *The Kaleidoscope of Care: A Review of Research on Welfare Provision for Elderly People*, HMSO

R Parker, I Sinclair and J Williams (1990), 'Financial Background', in I Sinclair, R Parker, D Leat and J Williams eds, *The Kaleidoscope of Care: A Review of Research on Welfare Provision for Elderly People*, HMSO

P Parsloe and O Stevenson (1993), *Community Care and Empowerment*, Joseph Rowntree Foundation

T Parsons (1951), *The Social System*, Tavistock

N Parry, M Rustin and C Satymurti eds (1979), *Social Work, Welfare and the State*, Edward Arnold

W Parry-Jones (1972), *The Trade in Lunacy*, Routledge and Kegan Paul

D Patrick and E Scrivens (1989), 'Allocating Resources to Meet Needs', in D Patrick and H Reach(eds), *Disablement in the Community*, Oxford University Press

B Perrin and B Nirje (1989), 'Setting the Record Straight: a Critique of Some Frequent Misconceptions of the Normalisation Principle', in A Brechin and J Walmsley eds, *Making Connections: Reflecting on the Lives and Experiences of People with Learning Difficulties*, Hodder and Stoughton

C Perring (1989), *Families Caring for those Diagnosed as Mentally Ill: a Literature Review*, University of York, Social Policy Research Unit Working Paper 484

N Pfieffer and A Coote (1991), *Is Quality Good for You? A Critical Review of Quality Assurance in Welfare Services*, Institute of Public Policy Research, Social Policy Paper No. 5

D Pilgrim (1993), *Community Care as Policy*, Open University, Workbook 2 of course K259, 'Community Care', Part 2

C Potrykus (1992), 'Paying the Price of Community Care', *Health Visitor*, Vol 65, No 3

P Power-Smith and M Evans (1992), 'Added Responsibility', *Community Care*, 29 August

Public Services Privatisation Research Unit (1993), *Report on the Community Care Policies of Local Authorities, Health Authorities and Boards*

H Qureshi (1990), 'Boundaries Between Formal and Informal Care Giving Work', in C Ungerson, ed, *Gender and Caring*, Harvester Wheatsheaf

S Ramon (1985), *Psychiatry in Britain: Meaning and Policy*, Croom Helm

S Ramon ed (1991a), *Beyond Community Care: Normalisation and Integration Work*, Macmillan

S Ramon (1991b), 'Principles and Conceptual Knowledge', in S Ramon ed, *Beyond Community Care: Normalisation and Integration Work*, Macmillan

J Read and J Wallcraft (1992), *Guidelines for Empowering Users of Mental Health Services*, COHSE/MIND Publications

D Redding (1989), 'An Eye on Procedures, but no Voice for Users', *Community Care*, 30 November, Special Supplement on the White Paper, *Caring for People*

G Ritzer (1993), *The McDonaldisation of Society*, Pine Forge Press

T Robinson (1989), 'Normalisation: the Whole Answer?' in A Brechin and J Walmsley eds, *Making Connections: Reflecting on the Lives and Experiences of People with Learning Difficulties*, Hodder and Stoughton

J Roebuck (1979), 'Where Does Old Age Begin? The Evolution of the English Definition', *Journal of Social History*, Vol 12, No 3

A Rogers and D Pilgrim (1991) '"Pulling Down Churches": Accounting for the British Mental Health Users' Movement', *Sociology of Health and Illness*

A Rogers, D Pilgrim and R Lacey (1992), *Experiencing Psychiatry: Users' Views of Services*, Macmillan

C Rogers (1978), *Carl Rogers on Personal Power*, Constable

R Rogers and J Salvage (1987), *Nurses at Risk: A Guide to Health and Safety at Work*, Heinemann

D Rothman (1971), *The Discovery of the Asylum*, Little, Brown and Co

J Ryan and F Thomas (1980), *The Politics of Mental Handicap*, Penguin (see also revised edition 1989)

M Rose (1972), *The Relief of Poverty 1834-1914*, Macmillan

Royal College of Psychiatrists (1993), *The Royal College Calls for an Amendment to the Mental Health Act 1983*, Press Release

A Scull (1979), *Museums of Madness*, Allen Lane

P Sedgwick (1982), *Psycho Politics*, Pluto

D Seedhouse (1986), *Health: the Foundations for Achievement*, John Wiley

M Sheppard (1990), 'Social Work and Community Psychiatric Nursing', in P Abbott and C Wallace eds, *The Sociology of the Caring Professions*, Falmer Press

E Showalter (1987), *The Female Malady*, Virago

I Sinclair and J Williams (1990), 'Demography, Health and Personal Resources', in I Sinclair, R Parker, D Leat and J Williams eds, *The Kaleidoscope of Care: A Review of Research on Welfare Provision for Elderly People*, HMSO

R Skellington and P Morris (1992), *Race in Britain Today*, Sage

V Skultans (1979), *English Madness: Ideas on Insanity 1580-1890*, Routledge and Kegan Paul

Socialist Health Association (1989), *Goodbye to All That?* (2nd edition)

Social Services Policy Forum (1992), *Who Owns Welfare?* National Institute of Social Work

M Soder (1984), 'The Mentally Retarded: Ideologies of Care and Surplus Population', in L Banton and S Tomlinson eds, *Special Education: Policy, Practice and Social Issues*, Croom Helm

K Sone (1990), 'At the Mercy of the Law', *Community Care*, 18 October

P Squires (1990), *Anti-Social Policy: Welfare, Ideology and the Disciplinary State*, Harvester Wheatsheaf

M Stacey, 'The Health Service Consumer: a Sociological Misconception', in M Stacey ed, *The Sociology of the National Health Service*, University of Keele, Sociological Review Monograph

G Stedman Jones (1971), *Outcast London*, Oxford University Press

D Stone (1984), *The Disabled State*, Macmillan

D Sudnow (1967), *Passing On, The Social Organisation of Dying*, Prentice Hall

T S Szasz (1961), *Ideology and Insanity*, New York, Doubleday

T S Szasz (1971), *The Manufacture of Madness*, Routledge and Kegan Paul

G Therborn (1989), 'The Two-Thirds, One-Third Society', in S Hall and M Jaques (eds), *New Times: the Changing Face of Politics in the 1990s*, Lawrence and Wishart

M Thomas (1993), *Community Care – A Report*, West Midlands Health Service Monitoring Unit

E P Thompson (1963), *The Making of the English Working Class*, Penguin

G Thornicroft et al (1993), 'Care Management and Mental Health', *British Medical Journal*, 20 March

R Titmuss (1968), 'Community Care: Fact or Fiction?' in *Commitment to Welfare*, George Allen and Unwin

M Titterton (1993), *Community Care Policy in the United Kingdom*, in Workbook 2 of Course K259 'Community Care', Open University, Appendix 2

D Tomlinson (1991), *Utopia, Community Care and the Retreat from Asylums*, Open University Press

D Tomlinson (1992), 'Life on the Outside', in *Health Matters: Community Health Reports*

B Tonkin (1987), 'Black and Blue', *Community Care*, 14 May

P Townsend (1962), *The Last Refuge*, Routledge and Kegan Paul

P Townsend (1973) 'The Political Sociology of Mental Handicap', in P Townsend, *The Social Minority*, Allen Lane

P Townsend (1979), *Poverty in the United Kingdom*, Penguin

P Townsend (1991-2), 'Hard Times', *European Labour Forum*, No.6, winter

P Townsend, N Davidson and M Whitehead (1988), *Inequalities in Health*, Penguin

K Tudor (1990/91), 'One Step Back, Two Steps Forward: Community Care and Mental Health', *Critical Social Policy*, Vol 10, No 3

A Tyne (1978), *Participation by Families of Mentally Handicapped People in Policy Making, London*, Personal Social Services Council

A Tyne (1982), 'Community Care and Mentally Handicapped People', in A Walker ed, *Community Care: the Family, State and Social Policy*, Basil Blackwell

J Ussher (1991), *Women's Madness: Misogyny or Mental Illness*, Harvester

C R Victor (1991), *Health and Health Care in Later Life*, Open University Press

L Warren (1990), 'We're Home Helps Because We Care', in P Abbot and G Payne eds, *New Directions in the Sociology of Health*, Falmer Press

G Wagner (1988), *Residential Care: a Positive Choice*, HMSO

A Walker (1982), 'The Meaning and Social Division of Community Care', in A Walker ed, *Community Care: the Family, the State and Social Policy*, Basil Blackwell

A Walker (1983), 'Social Policy and Elderly People in Great Britain: the Construction of Dependent Social and Economic Status in Old Age', in A-M Guillemard ed, *Old Age and the Welfare State*, Sage

A Walker (1989), 'Community Care', in M McCarthy ed, *The New Politics of Welfare: an Agenda for the 1990s?*, Macmillan

A Walker (1993), 'Community Care Policy: from Consensus to Conflict', in J
Bornat et al, eds, *Community Care: a Reader*, Macmillan

J Walmsley and F Williams (1990), 'Transitions and Change', Workbook 3
of Open University Course K668, *Mental Handicap: Changing Perspectives*

M Wicks (1982), 'Community Care and Elderly People', in A Walker ed,
*Community Care: the Family, the State and Social Policy*, Basil Blackwell and
Martin Robertson

P Wilding (1981), *Socialism and the Professions*, Fabian Tract 473

P Wilding (1982), *Professional Power and Social Welfare*, Routledge and Kegan
Paul

F Williams (1989a), *Social Policy: a Critical Introduction*, Polity Press

F Williams (1989b), 'Mental Handicap and Oppression', in *Making Connections: Reflecting on the Lives and Experiences of People with Learning Difficulties*,
Hodder and Stoughton

R Williams (1975), *The Country and The City*, Paladin

R Williams and B Shoultz (1982), *We Can Speak for Ourselves*, Souvenir Press

E Wilson (1977), *Women and the Welfare State*, Tavistock

M Wing (1992), 'Sorry – No Work Today, Nurse...', *Health Matters*, Summer

P Winterton (1938), *Mending Minds*, Victor Gollancz

G Wistow (1988), 'Off-loading Responsibilities for Care', in R Maxwell ed,
*Reshaping the National Health Service*, Transaction Books

G Wistow (1990), *Community Care Planning: A Review of Past Experiences and
Future Imperatives*, Department of Health

G Wistow, I Leedham and B Hardy (1993a), *Preliminary Analysis of a Sample of
English Community Care Plans*, Department of Health

G Wistow, I Leedham and B Hardy (1993b), 'Planning Blight', *Community
Care*, 18 February

W Wolfensberger (1972), *The Principles of Normalisation in Human Services*,
Toronto, National Institute on Mental Retardation

W Wolfensberger (1983), 'Social Role Valorisation: a Proposed New Term
for the Principle of Normalisation', *Mental Retardation*, Vol 21 No 6,
pp.234-9

W Wolfensberger and S Tullman (1989), 'A Brief Outline of the Principle of
Normalisation', in A Brechin and J Walmsley eds, *Making Connections: Reflecting on the Lives of People with Learning Difficulties*, Hodder and
Stoughton

K Woolf, D P Goldberg, and T Fryers (1988), 'The Practice of Community
Psychiatric Nursing and Mental Health Social Work in Salford: Some Implications for Community Care', *British Journal of Psychiatry*, Vol 152

K Woolf and D P Goldberg (1988), 'Further Observations on the Practice of
Community Care in Salford: Differences Between Community Psychiatric
Nurses and Mental Health Social Workers', *British Journal of Psychiatry*, Vol
153

E O Wright and D Cho (1992), 'State Employment, Class Location and Ideological Orientation: a Comparative Analysis of the United States and
Sweden', *Politics and Society*, Vol 20, No 2.

K Wright (1990), *Creating a Market in Social Care: the Problems for Community
Care*, Centre for Health Economics, York

# Index